MASALA CHAI
for the SOUL

Jairam N. Menon is a communications consultant. He began his professional career as a sub-editor with *The Free Press Journal* before joining the advertising and PR department of a leading engineering and construction company. He is a writer whose versatility straddles journalism, advertising and corporate communications. The seeds for this book were sown in a column he used to write for the in-house magazine of a leading engineering and construction company, which also proved to be the reader's favourite section.

He has lived in Mumbai since the time it was known as Bombay and calls the madding city the only home he knows.

Connect with the author at
https://twitter.com/JairamKJairam

'Jairam has brewed a great cup of tea with some amazing masala ingredients. Every sip or every chapter makes you think anew about a problem that you may have encountered and then makes you smile. Pick up this book, brew some masala tea and enjoy both with some salty snacks.'

—**Ambi Parameswaran**
Brand Strategy Coach and Bestselling Author

'Crackling wit, a droll voice and astute observations on the truisms of life, this is an absolute must-read. One of those books you dip into over and over again in the vain hope of a nugget you perchance missed.'

—**Kiran Manral**
Author

'Hilariously tongue-in-cheek, I loved it, and it made enormous sense even though I have no boss and attend no office. Thanks for writing this book!'

—**Naseeruddin Shah**
Actor

'We are told to take seriously life, vocation, avocation, relationships, and every possible influence on us. That is absolutely correct.

We are also told NOT to take too seriously life, vocation, avocation, relationships and every influence. That is also correct. When we are confused, we are told to find the balance. Hell, how do you find that mythical balance?

Read this book.'

—**R. Gopalakrishnan**
Author and Corporate Advisor

'Jairam Menon breaks the rules, busts the myths and does it in an enjoyable, conversational style.'

—**Vir Sanghvi**
Writer and Columnist

MASALA CHAI
for the SOUL

How to brew this, that and everything else

JAIRAM N. MENON
Foreword by **BACHI KARKARIA**

Published by
Rupa Publications India Pvt. Ltd 2024
7/16, Ansari Road, Daryaganj
New Delhi 110002

Sales centres:
Bengaluru Chennai
Hyderabad Jaipur Kathmandu
Kolkata Mumbai Prayagraj

Text and illustrations copyright © Jairam N. Menon 2024
Foreword copyright © Bachi Karkaria 2024

Some parts of this book were first published by *The Hindu*.

The views and opinions expressed in this book
are the author's own and the facts are as reported by him,
which have been verified to the extent possible,
and the publishers are not in any way liable for the same.

All rights reserved.

No part of this publication may be reproduced, transmitted
or stored in a retrieval system, in any form or by any means,
electronic, mechanical, photocopying, recording or otherwise,
without the prior permission of the publisher.

P-ISBN: 978-93-5702-723-6
E-ISBN: 978-93-5702-739-7

First impression 2024

10 9 8 7 6 5 4 3 2 1

The moral right of the author has been asserted.

Printed in India

This book is sold subject to the condition that it shall not, by way of
trade or otherwise, be lent, resold, hired out or otherwise circulated,
without the publisher's prior consent, in any form of binding or cover
other than that in which it is published.

To P.N. Menon and Sita Menon

*This book is dedicated to my parents,
both no more.
In their distinctive ways,
they added a sunbeam to my life.*

*To my dad,
from whom I inherited the quirky gene.
He used to tell me there is a funny side
to almost everything in life.
He said it even as he lay in the hospital
(his last day in the hospital was also his first).
2024 is his birth centenary,
and I can't think of a better present
that would make him happier.
My first fan—he will remain my most special one.*

*And to my mother,
who stood by disapprovingly
as I began working on the manuscript.
She told me to do something more worthwhile
than writing a book that nobody was going to read.
I hope I can prove her wrong, at least this once.*

Contents

Foreword by Bachi Karkaria   ix
Introduction   xi

1. Save the World. Do Nothing.   1
2. Love thy Enemies—and May their Tribe Increase   5
3. Eco-friendly, Politically-correct Protests   10
4. Let Fine Art, Fellini and the Philharmonic Drive Your Career   14
5. Happily, in the Middle   20
6. Company for the Lonely   24
7. The Good Thing about Gossip   28
8. Absent-minded? Forget it.   32
9. Envy-Proofing Your Life   36
10. Dealing with People You Don't Like   40
11. Fussing about Cussing   47
12. Where There's a Bill, There's a Way   52
13. Know Your Bore Score   55
14. Ageing Happily and Wisely   59
15. Yes, No…a Definite Maybe   63
16. Killing Yourself to Stay Fit   67
17. Cooking Up Corporate Statements   71
18. Fool is Cool   75
19. Touch Wood, Chashmebaddoor!   79
20. No Sin Being Cynics   83
21. Flying High in Borrowed Feathers   87
22. Facing a 'Firing'   91

23. Worrying Works Wonders	95
24. The Tyranny of Thought	99
25. Small Talk, The Social Lubricant	103
26. Murthy's Law	107
27. 'Please Adjust'	111
28. 'A' is for the Average	115
29. Making the Party Work for You	119
30. 9 to 5	123
31. The Fine Art of Flattery	126
32. .Life's a Bargain	131
33. God Help Us with Our Faith!	135
34. A Toast to the Boast!	139
35. Unplugging Nostalgia	144
36. Procrastination versus Anti-crastination	148
37. Do Less, Delegate More	153
38. All Hail the Excuse	157
39. Managing Your Boss	161
40. Playing the Name Game	165
41. Life Lessons from Potholes	169
42. The Bald, Bold and Beautiful	174
43. No Spitting, Know Spitting	177
44. Becoming an Expert	181
45. Dealing with 'Meeting-itis'	186
46. Getting Wise to Good Advice	190
47. Sleeping on the Job	193
48. Winning the 'Cold' War	197
49. Minding our Ps and Queues	201
50. In Praise of Praise	205
51. And Finally...	209
Acknowledgements	210

FOREWORD

From 'Backword' to this Foreword, I've come a long way with Jairam Menon. *Masala Chai for the Soul* proves that he's come a longer way than when I gingered up the pieces that he submitted for the section we started on the back page of *The Times of India*, Bombay (now Mumbai), some 30 years ago. He belonged to the stuffy world of business suits, but even then, it was refreshing to find that 'full many a gem […] the dark unfathom'd [depts. of corporate] oceans bear'.

This book is self-help laced with wit and stripped of the usual patronizing. There's a great need for its ilk today when we all suffocate under the shrink-wrap of stress. The irony is that the one-pill-suits-all advice dispensed by Inner-Calmness quacks is as short-term a solution as an over-the-counter aspirin.

'Doctor' Menon promises less and delivers more. He's injected humour into the thickened veins of everyday anxieties and fears, needling 'received wisdom' and syringing out the grimness that infects all pop panaceas. This book counsels against self-flagellation every time we make a fool of ourselves; fall fast asleep in public; indulge occasionally in bitchy, no-holds-barred gossip; forget what our spouses told us; or cheat on our gym sessions—sloth triumphs over iron resolve. It also comes with survival kits for a variety of composure-threatening situations ranging from the boss's unreasonable outburst to being tongue-tied when you want the impressing words to flow or even the BP-raising annoyance of always being the last in a very long, very slow queue.

Masala Chai for the Soul is a contrarian's canon, so standard Dos and Don'ts are upended. A few dreams are deflated too. But then, you can't have masala without some heartburn.

From Jairam's early pieces, I suspected that he was a covert anarchist. I'm glad he's come out of the closet. No greater need than now for mirth-spiked Molotov cocktails.

—**Bachi Karkaria**
Columnist and Bestselling Author

INTRODUCTION

Life Hacks for Easier Living

First, take a meditative sip of masala chai.

As you slurp your way ahead, slowly the fog will clear and help you find the answers you seek.

You are looking to find Meaning and Purpose in Life, Attain Contentment, Inner Peace, Deeper Understanding, etc. In short, you want this, that and everything else. But, how do you get what you want? Well, start laughing—at this, that and everything else!

Laughter, the *Reader's Digest* had told us long ago, is the best medicine. That could have been then. Today, it's much more. It is your co-conspirator in dealing with life, your escape route, your safety valve and Plan B; it is useful to bring down the temperature in human interactions and cool the planet; it is a relationship builder and diffuser of conflicts. Most of all, as in my case, it is the safeguard of sanity.

What do you laugh at? There's a big spread:

1. Laugh at the twists and turns life takes.
2. Laugh because you could be down one day, and plunge deeper the next.
3. Laugh because life is not a game, it's a circus, and the world is neither round nor flat, it is obtuse.
4. Laugh at masks—the ones you can't see.
5. Laugh at humbug passing off as profundity.
6. Laugh at relationships that are prey to circumstance.

7. Laugh at statements of belief that are part pretence, part PR.
8. Laugh at eloquence that masks ignorance, and at the arrogance that does the same.
9. Laugh at ostentatious piety that won't stand the test of scrutiny.
10. Laugh at the charity that lacks the large-heartedness of generosity.
11. Laugh at the petty thievery we punish, and the larceny we glorify.
12. Laugh at self-centredness that is all-consuming.
13. Laugh at louts pretending to be gentlefolk.
14. Laugh at principles that succumb so readily to opportunity.
15. Laugh at the scheming and conniving, which occupy the better part of our days.
16. Laugh at the earnestness with which we deceive ourselves.
17. Laugh at the hypocrisies that we have internalized.
18. Laugh at timidity masquerading as virtue.
19. Laugh at the truth that is fed to us, and at the fakery we consume.
20. Laugh at conventions that have become constraints.
21. Laugh at your accomplishments as much as at your inadequacies.
22. Laugh at those who laugh at you.
23. And most of all, whatever the circumstance, don't forget to laugh at yourself.

This book is for you, *not* because it will get you to your destination faster (it probably won't) or set you in the *right* direction (that depends on how well you read maps) but because it will make the journey called *life* bearable, and the fare is cheap (you get the gyaan from a lot of books for the price of one). And if nothing else, you would have had a nice cup of tea.

Save the World. Do Nothing.

Shirkers of the world, unite! There's a lot to be done...
or rather, be left undone.

For many people, 'lazy' is a four-letter word, generally clubbed with lout, loser, slouch and good-for-nothing…a Shashi Tharoor may chip in with 'ne'er do well'. Sadly, you are not likely to hear anyone from the opposite camp springing spiritedly to its defence. That's not because we have nothing to say; it's just that we are too damn lazy.

I can understand where these vigorous, vociferous, anti-lazy lobbyists are coming from—they are coming from the caves. Back in the day, when all men were hunters and gatherers, the slacker who neither hunted bravely nor gathered assiduously but better occupied his time on the Paleolithic version of WhatsApp, was a blot on the social landscape, a dangerous role model who could push the tribe to deprivation and death. The ages that followed have been no kinder to the do-littles of the world. But it was the Industrial Age when every available hand was needed to keep the engines of the economy firing, which put a halo around hard labour and spawned a social stigma around lethargy. But those days are long past us. Unfortunately, the world's workaholics have been too busy at the office to notice.

Religious leaders seem to be hand in glove with managers, mukadams and mothers-in-law, creating conditions that make hard work seem an exalted virtue. Society expects us to not only work long hours but also every minute of those hours. It takes someone like Alexis Ohanian, co-founder of Reddit, to say, 'The idea that unless you are suffering, grinding, working every hour of every day, you are not working hard enough… is one of the most dangerous things in tech right now.'

The fact is, there is too much work being done today, and most of it is of the wrong kind. It is time that the patron saint of sloth reappears to show people the light. Far from being a social menace, the 'disinclination to work of any kind', as Jerome K. Jerome put it, may just be the thing to help us get out of the mess we are in. Imagine wannabe scamsters plotting to embezzle the bank in which lie your life's savings. They plough through the bank's standard operating procedures, spend painstaking hours forging documents to precision and proceed to set up shell companies in Mauritius and the Cayman Islands, which will clinch the deal. They are tired and feel they need a break. Suddenly, out of the corner of their eyes, they catch a glimpse of the azure sea, the golden sand and the welcoming hammocks. They look at each other, shrug and decide that they deserve a break, and…stress-test the said hammocks. What happens with this blatant act of shirking work? The bank escapes ruin and your money stays safe.

Or take leaders of incipient lynch mobs, or potential suicide bombers who yield to the heady charms of lazing around and put off their respective tasks by another hour, another day, another week…it's the laggards who will save our world.

There is something endearingly human about those who can doze off in the teeth of pressing deadlines. Eager beavers who copiously burn the midnight oil lose no opportunity to tell the world about their work schedule—lest their efforts go unnoticed, and therefore, un-praised. But you will never hear idlers boasting about the long hours they spent stretching on the armchair because they are not looking to score points off you. We all know of people who slog away at home and the office just to make the rest of us feel bad. The easy-goer resorts to no such blackmail. When money talks and power proclaims, he is among the few who don't form part of the respectful audience.

Rest assured, our idle minds are far from being the devil's

workshop. Honestly, we slouches can't put a Lego set together, let alone operate a workshop. Instead, we can help soothe nerves frazzled by deadlines and 'To Do' lists, safeguard you from karoshi (Japanese for death due to overwork) and come up with productivity boosters, like a power snooze (an officially sanctioned nap for everyone from grand-aunts to general managers and government servants) or pixel meditation—the technique of staring with great concentration at your computer screen, convincing everyone around that you are deeply immersed in work even as your mind reprises the World Cup. An equally effective labour-saving tool is procrastination. Putting things off for tomorrow works wonders because if you ignore problems for long enough, they usually sort themselves out in the end.

Management consultants seem to have made a fetish of 'multitasking'—the overrated ability of celebrity housewives and smart executives to do many things simultaneously and successfully. It makes me wonder if these consultants actually know what's going on around them. Out there, the real world is complaining of rising unemployment. Clearly, then, the need of the hour is to avoid doing as many things as possible so that there are enough jobs left to go around. We 'multi-shirkers' are society's real assets; we don't take away other people's jobs. In fact, we would love it if somebody would take away ours!

If you want to start a movement to promote public health, lasting peace and universal happiness, enlist idlers. Then, tell them to go ahead and do what they do best—nothing.

> 'It is impossible to enjoy idling thoroughly unless one has plenty of work to do.'
>
> —Jerome K. Jerome

Love thy Enemies—and May their Tribe Increase

Enemies can't betray you; they won't disappoint you
and they don't bore the pants off you.
Yet they hardly ever get good press.

Every morning, there are a million posts going around the web, wishing the time of the day, dripping with the syrupy virtues of friendship, love, bonding and other stuff so cringeworthy that it would make characters in an Ekta Kapoor serial seem stoic. Events like Friendship Day (the first Sunday of August) trigger such a sugary tsunami, that if the internet was borderline diabetic, you could bet it would have lapsed into a coma.

But look at things through the cold prism of reason, and you will see a world suffering from the debilitating effects of an animosity deficit. The inconvenient truth is that the human species needs enemies as much as, if not more than, it needs friends.

Let's suppose we want to know the truth about ourselves. We certainly can't depend on our friends for it. Most of us rate our own abilities and achievements quite highly and we believe that if we are not already rich and famous, it's solely because the world is slow to recognize and reward our special kind of talent. Your chums—well-meaning but undiscerning—tend to go along with these assessments, and counting on them to give you an objective opinion about yourself is as unlikely as expecting Katappa to backstab Baahubali. So if you want the facts without the fluff, it's best to consult your nearest enemy.

An enemy at the gate is also useful as a cohesive force. At its core, humanity is essentially a motley, uneasy bunch of leftists, rightists, humanists, centrists, extremists, atheists, fundamentalists and all manner of 'ists', including the odd nudist, á la Ranveer Singh. Left to ourselves, we will scheme and squabble, bicker and backstab at the slightest opportunity. History shows that nothing prevents society from splintering along pre-existing fault lines as effectively as a figure or an issue we can all hate in unison.

As long as the British were strutting around their colonies, we knew where to lay the blame for everything that was going wrong. After Independence, those niggling little things we could not stand about each other (earlier subsumed under the greater dislike for the British yoke) spluttered to the surface. The results are what you see in the papers every day.

Indians with long memories will remember that in the early 1960s, the anti-Hindi agitation had assumed ominous undertones with strident talk of Tamil Nadu seceding from the nation. Just when things were looking as if they would go out of hand, a foe helpfully showed up at our borders, viz., China (like leopards, the Chinese don't change their spots). When they overran our frontier posts, the flamboyant M.G. Ramachandran announced the withdrawal of the agitation, saying he did not want to pave the way for the enemy, and chipped in with a handsome donation to the Armed Forces fund. The tide turned, and although the issue kept cropping up at predictable intervals, it could never muster the same vintage virulence. The Chinese have reason to be miffed that we did not thank them enough for helping our country sort out its internal problems.

Enlightened souls, holy men and philosophers, of course, have a different take on the subject. They are all for cosying up to your enemies, and either getting them to see things from your point of view or adjusting your own perspective to suit theirs. Against the weight of their combined counsel, I would pit Ronda Rousey. Her CV does not describe her as a philosopher of any standing, but she is the former bantamweight champion of mixed martial arts (so you disagree at your peril). And she has said: 'Fighting is good for society's health.' If you believe Ronda is more brawn than brain, let's push farther back in history and go higher up the intellectual scale. Hazlitt, the eighteenth-century essayist weighed in with: 'Love turns, with little indulgence, to indifference or disgust; hatred alone is immortal.' Better still, just rerun an old Hollywood epic. In William Wyler's *Ben-Hur*, you will hear the Roman Consul Quintus Arrius whipping the hero in the ship's galley, and then telling him: 'Hate keeps a man alive.'

Look back at your life. It's generally the enemy who brings out the best in us. Our adrenaline—that wonder juice that turns the average into the excellent—is opponent-dependent. In the office, a sworn rival in the next cabin can do wonders for our efficiency—more effective than a roomful of friends shouting encouragement. They sharpen our responses and prompt us to go the extra mile. After all, we don't want to let the dastard next door get promoted before us, do we?

At the social level too, enemies perform a useful function: they keep the conversation crackling. Try this at your next get-together. Set the ball rolling with a savoury character sketch of the target—the upstart staying upstairs, your club president, his overweening secretary…anyone will do (provided, of course, they are not among those present). Serving up an enemy for the evening is like announcing that the bar is open. Suddenly, the atmosphere perks up and everyone readies for a good time. Friends will contribute their own perspectives about so-and-so and some will add rib-tickling sidelights. Before you know it, a lacklustre assembly turns into a rollicking, high-decibel event.

If our B-schools really knew what's good for their students in later life, they would begin teaching 'Enemy Management'. And the first lesson will be on how to pick the right enemy. You need to be careful—more careful, in fact, than when picking friends.

At the global level, America has long been a popular enemy—as universal a staple as daal chawal. You could lay the blame for virtually everything on America, whether for internal strife (US-funded), for our troubles with Pakistan (instigated by US arms manufacturers) or for our cultural decadence (too obvious to need explanation). But the Americans now have serious competition. There's Russia under the unsmiling Mr Putin, and China under the seemingly congenitally constipated Xi Jinping. There are also religious fundamentalists who are racing up the charts and rapidly emerging as everyone's favourite foe. Other standard options in India include netas of all stripes, the media, a certain anchor, the builder lobby, the drug mafia and the 'other' community... The menu is long and you should certainly find a flavour you like.

The fact is our minds are so wired and hearts so structured that we need to hate, almost as much as we need to love. If we don't find a suitable enemy, we will, God forbid, begin to hate our friends.

So thank your stars for your enemies.

'Forgive your enemies, but never forget their names.'

—John F. Kennedy

Eco-friendly, Politically-correct Protests

*If a picture is worth a thousand words,
an expressive face is worth a thousand pictures.*

Let's face it. There are so many things wrong with this great big world of ours that if you were to rely on mainstream methods of protesting, you would run out of stones to pelt, placards to hold up or palatial presidential offices to storm. Heck, you won't even have snarky things left to say on social media. This doesn't mean you don't protest—doing nothing would be 'sinning by silence' as the popular, if wildly misattributed, quote goes. The solution then is to follow my advice and look for innovative ways of expressing the dissent of man. I've hit upon a method that is based on the fundamental assumption that emojis speak louder than epithets. It's low-decibel, non-violent and deeply satisfying. I make faces.

Last evening, when the autorickshaw driver refused to take me on the short, 21-rupee-ride home, I thought it unwise, even juvenile, to argue the point with him. Instead, stepping outside his line of vision, I mirrored the fellow's cussedness by puffing up my cheeks and pulling my lips down. Bolstered by the response from passers-by, I went so far as to wink conspiratorially at my newly-won fans. Such ready audience feedback is among the prized benefits of practising face farce—the noble art of publicly, or sometimes, privately, turning those who you wish to target into figures of fun. Face farce also helps keep your emotions in check. Even if you are blessed with a calm temperament, the strain of trying to never lose your temper can make you irritable. A funny face is your safety valve, and immediate relief is guaranteed.

I think most people have not yet realized the potential that literally lies under their noses. Think of the many character defects you can highlight without saying a word: your boss' pomposity, your neighbour's thrift and self-centredness, your aunt's avarice or the mulish nature of the traffic cop at the signal. Some of your best faces could well be the spontaneous outcome of an exasperating situation. Pull a lazy-Joe face at the lethargic clerk at the bank, and you not only avenge the delay you have been subjected to but also win friends along the queue. The best part is that it can all be done with easy-to-learn adjustments of your facial muscles—a pull here, a stretch there and a wicked twist. If you are high on imagination and low on inhibition, the field is all yours.

This is where the face artist scores over those vocal votaries of speaking up. Free speech, assuming it exists these days, comes with caveats that can cramp your style. There are limits to what you can say or do to others before libel, assault and battery laws come into play. Facial expressions, however, slip quietly under the radar. For instance, it's not socially acceptable to greet pesky telemarketers by showering them with vile (if well-deserved) comments about them and their forefathers. But there's nothing in the book to stop you from launching into a lively interplay of furrowed brows, pouting lips and tilted jaws while engaging with them.

These days, our tolerance threshold for verbal abuse and boyish horseplay is low, and getting lower still. Let's say you bop someone on the head; he is going to bop you back. It's a matter of time then, before bops turn to blows, and blows turn to blood feuds that extend across many generations. All this can be prevented if you content yourself with a spate of nasty faces, and he responds in kind. When you are done, you can both have a good laugh and go your separate ways.

Shabash! You have just done your bit for world peace.

Once this form of protest graduates into a performing art, I am sure we are going to witness sweeping social change. When the argumentative Indian turns into a vividly expressive one (less Amartya Sen and more Mr Bean), we can begin to enjoy zero-decibel debates in Parliament, state assemblies and television shows. You won't need to flinch as TV panellists try and cow each other down with blood-curdling war cries. Just sit back and amuse yourself as they curve their lips into a snarl, bare their incisors and cross their eyes. Will any of this make a meaningful political point? Well, ask yourself, do some of your most watched TV channels do any better?

As and when face farce enters our homes, it should put an end to that infuriating narration of your shortcomings and errors, a.k.a. nagging. You look at your spouse and the spouse stares back, all without a word being exchanged. This rosy picture of domestic bliss will only be tinged with the wall-to-wall scowls that you may need to put up with. But be reasonable, you can't ask for everything in life.

And here's one final word of counsel. If you don't like

what you have been reading in these pages so far, don't bother with the elaborate formality of burning this book along with the effigy of the author. You will experience the same sense of satisfaction if you turn your nose up, roll your pupils towards the ceiling and let your tongue hang out sideways. That way everyone is happy.

> 'Seriousness is a disease.'
>
> —Osho

Let Fine Art, Fellini and the Philharmonic Drive Your Career

Making sure your culture quotient keeps pace with your career graph.

There are plenty of self-help books that tell you how to 'think' your way to success. There are ways to meditate and become 'mindful'. And there are workout sessions that show you how to subtract inches from your waist and transfer them to your biceps. What none of them reveal is the subtler nuances of becoming refined, and boosting your 'soft power'. Now, I won't go along with those who say that the only culture we used to know was agriculture and that currently, the 'three R's' taught in schools is all about the film that was the toast of the Oscars. That's obviously not true. But it's only of late that people have begun to appreciate the deep correlation between culture and your career graph, between art and your next increment. So here, by the grace of the entire pantheon, from Sonal Mansingh to Sanjay Roy, is your shortcut to cultural nirvana.

All learning begins with a spell of unlearning. Your first lesson, therefore, is to jettison the esoteric pursuits of your youthful days. You may have once delighted in Ram Gopal Varma's films. Himesh Reshammiya may have given voice to your soul. And you may think the world of calendar art is far prettier than the absurdly contoured Anish Kapoor installation everyone is drooling over. But steel yourself for change. As you step onto the escalator of success, it is time to bid your old friends a firm goodbye.

Roughly above the rank of assistant manager, the Kumars and Khans should be deposed from your list of favourites and Godard or Fellini installed in their place. Who in God's name is Godard and who the you-know-what is Fellini? Both were European filmmakers who have given the world a somewhat taxing body of work—you can Google them for more details (I just did and learnt that Godard, God rest his soul, passed away recently). But don't get into specifics. If someone asks you who Godard was, affect stunned surprise that they don't know him. That will keep them off your back.

At any elite gathering of executives, a discussion about the profound 'dialogues' of RRR or the sledgehammer sentiment of an Ekta Kapoor serial is as unwelcome as a cuss word in an early morning bhajan. In fact, above a certain grade, let alone local fare, even talking about Hollywood is inadvisable if you want to awaken your inner Anupama Chopra and hop on to the fast track to promotion. You should instead be talking about 'mise-en-scène' and 'montage'. What's mise-en-scène? Again, don't waste time looking for answers. You can bet that films from Poland, Iran and Japan have mise-en-scène in spades.

So a good conversation opener when wannabe VPs get together would be: 'Kurosawa's handling of the warrior archetype is deft. Ah, and the imagery is oblique and yet so compelling.' Your listeners—fellow managers and above—may not exactly understand what the hell you are driving at but will be sensible enough to nod their heads.

Also, you will soon discover that you don't have to actually see the movies you say you admire. All you need to do is read the reviews in the papers. You needn't feel guilty about this discreet practice. After all, when there are professional film reviewers getting paid to watch intensely cerebral East European films, it makes sense to utilize their services to the full. If you still feel bad, take a leaf from Hemingway's *The Old Man and the Sea*. The central character quelled self-doubt by simply saying to himself: 'Do not think about sin […] there are people who are paid to do it. Let them think about it.'

Sooner or later, the fast-rising executive will have to contend with an 'agni pariksha', or the formal luncheon or dinner. You will think this is going to be fun since fine wine and food prepared by chefs with Michelin stars sprinkled in their resumes will be on offer. But there is literally many a slip between the cup and your lip. So here's a statutory warning: you are being watched, and if you spill cream over the table cloth, use the crab spoon for the soufflé, pronounce Pinot Noir to rhyme with 'Nair' or, horror of horrors, plonk your elbows up on the table, you are immediately slotted as a 'low life'. But despair not. Salvation arrives in the form of being forewarned and therefore forearmed. There are simple instructions on dining etiquette available on the net. You also need to spend just a couple of weeks familiarizing yourself with French and American cuisines on MasterChef. With practice you could pass off as a gourmand. You can even go a step further and become the connoisseur-with-a-conscience by politely declining the pâté foie gras (it shows that you know how it is made).

Soon, it will be time for you to literally face the music. As a hotshot executive who has been marked out by senior management for higher responsibilities, you are expected to attend lofty music recitals (the less they sound like Himesh Reshammiya, the loftier they are). Don't get unnerved when your office gives you tickets for a philharmonic orchestra that is fresh out of Vienna.

The first two things to learn about classical music are how to not fall asleep when the conductor is in mid-flight and how to not let your head sink into your chest or topple onto the nearest chiffon-clad shoulder. Put your head to more useful purposes—like nodding it in time with the music. Then...

when you sense from the groundswell of reactions around you that the music is reaching a phase of extreme poignancy, sit up and twirl your fingers, as Sri Lanka's unforgettable Muttiah Muralitharan used to when dishing out the doosra. You will soon be the envy of the less cognizant occupying the cheaper seats at the back.

From concerts, you next plot your strategy for the canvas. Now, this is going to be tougher than the rest because modern art has no rules to help tell a masterpiece from a mishmash. Even connoisseurs need to be careful to not be caught with their pants down. Recently, in Europe, museum curator Susanne Meyer-Buser discovered that Dutch painter Piet Mondrian's greatly admired masterpiece had, for seventy-five years, been hanging upside down in a museum. But that hadn't stopped art lovers from admiring it anyhow.

Perplexing as modern art can be, guile and daring should see you through. Begin by taking take time off one weekend to study provenances. That has nothing to do with the form or colour of the painting but with a record of its ownership and authenticity. It is going to be boring work, but bear with us. Persistence pays. You should also be able to recognize artists by their signatures. Once you are able to distinguish a Souza scrawl from a Husain squiggle, you are ready to face the world. When your corporate host next takes you along to view his company's art collection, you should be ready with your moves. Don't come up with the usual, 'Oh, how lovely!' (That will get you only a 'C'.) Instead, pause silently for a while, as if overawed, stoop low (in both the literal and metaphorical sense) until you catch the artist's name, and say: 'Husain's whimsicality never deserted him. His oeuvre (pronounced *ooh-vruh*) teemed with mischief.' You can bet your host will wish that he had said this himself, and you will have risen in his esteem.

There is just one touch needed to complete the picture—the book you carry around. If your favourite reading is, let's call a spade a spade, the *Playboy Annual*—don't stop reading, let's just tuck the volume out of sight. The kind of books that win respect and promotion are this year's winners of the International Booker Prize or the Nobel Prize in Literature. If you are feeling adventurous, sweep all Anglo-American writers aside (everybody's reading them), and get infatuated with novelists from lesser-known lands, like Nigeria, Hungary and Chile. If you are working in a public sector organization, and it is 'Hindi Week', it would be a good idea to add the first Hindi International Booker Prize winner, *Tomb of Sand*, to the tomes you carry around. Our honourable Home Minister will be ecstatic if you call it *Ret Samadhi* and actually manage to complete the noble work.

Finally, after you have run the gauntlet of high art, music and culture, you face the ultimate question. How do you tell everyone that you have arrived? Well, years ago, in the eponymous film *Sagina*, the immortal thespian chose to announce to the world that he had made it big with '*Saala Main Toh Sahab Ban Gaya...*!'

Look it up on YouTube and belt out the number. You can't put it better than Dilip Kumar.

> 'Give me the right word and the right accent and I will move the world.'
>
> —Joseph Conrad

Happily, in the Middle

In the tug-of-war between the rich and the poor, the middle class plays the rope.

Let's face it. The middle class is a bit of neither here nor there, neither fish nor fowl, neither neighbour's envy nor owner's pride. Politicians pass us over, having instinctively and accurately divined that it is the poor who will fetch them votes, and the rich who will give them the moolah. The media can't be bothered. They romanticize the poor and they go into raptures over the excesses of the affluent, at whose wedding parties high society dances itself silly. But what about the people in between—the millions like you and I? The inconvenient truth is, we don't make a good story.

Or don't we? Perhaps a bit of misplaced modesty has stood in the way of us getting our due. We, the middle class or 'MC' (no relative of the popular swear word), ought to get a public service medal for just being who we are. Here's a much-delayed citation:

We belong to close-knit neighbourhoods and even closer-knit families. We make perfect 'people next door'—give or take the occasional squabble over parking or the racket that the kids make in the common lobby. Neighbours in tony Malabar Hill in Mumbai and their counterparts in other metropolitan cities don't meet each other for months and are strangers for all practical purposes. But come down to the less snooty suburbs and things get far chummier.

In Andheri, my neighbours know me; my daily routine, my state of health and my state of wealth. If you start chatting with them, they will even tell you how things stand between me and my in-laws. All this means that the spectre of loneliness, which looms before the inhabitants of the world's big cities, doesn't scare us. You are never alone if you are in Andheri, especially in Chakala.

We, MCs, also score high on honesty, integrity and assorted virtues. The masterminds of big money crimes—embezzling banks, running Ponzi schemes or gaming the system are millionaires attempting to become billionaires. There is only one role that MCs play in all these financial scams: we are the whimpering victims. We also go scrupulously by the book when paying our taxes. Now, saying that middle-class morality is a default virtue because most of our dues are in any case deducted at source is being mean-spirited. There have been occasions where we claim leave travel allowance, while not stirring out of our homes, submit spurious medical certificates or seek reimbursements for taxi fare when we have actually commuted by autorickshaw. But those are exceptions. As a whole, our copybook is as clean as a Swachh Bharat advertisement.

Our brand image is worth its weight in gold. You can pity the poor. And you can call the rich names—crass ('there's no culture in the kitty party crowd'), heartless ('they torture their maids') and patriotism-deficient ('they go on vacations when they ought to be voting'), but nobody has an unkind word for us. That's why everyone jumps in to lay claim to possessing the sturdy values of the middle class. In fact, the biographies of men and women who are now both opulent and corpulent invariably begin their tale by recalling the good old days when they were *just* middle-class citizens.

A recent recruit to these ranks is ad man Piyush Pandey. In *Pandeymonium*, he says that it was his MC upbringing in Rajasthan that brought him in touch with vegetable vendors, carpenters, dhobis, tailors, mochis, et al. He actually talked to the tradesfolk rather than dealing with them through the serried ranks of servants. They told him evocative stories about their lives, and little Pandey filed away the highlights for later use, as award winners in advertising.

As we speak, the rich are rapidly getting richer and the poor poorer. Avant-garde French economist Thomas Piketty has said that as long as the returns on capital are higher than the rate of economic growth, the gap between the classes will widen. This means that we in the middle have an even bigger role in the increasingly fierce social tug of war. If it wasn't for our noble work, the haves and the have-nots, the super-haves and the never-hads would all go their separate ways, like a mahagathbandhan gone phut.

Since the middle class is contributing so much to keeping society intact, isn't it time we asked that we be paid for our services—preferably with oodles of cash transferred to an account in Lichtenstein? Ah, tempting...but that would go against our grain. No ill-gotten gains for us, guys. Please continue deriving happiness from the things that money can't buy, and keeping faith in Ruskin Bond's prescription for happiness—a mysterious thing to be found somewhere between too much and too less.

In old Hindi films of the Raj Kapoor and K.A. Abbas vintage, we all knew that the toiling farmer was, at the end of the day, more content than the wealthy and generally sleazy zamindar. But that was then. In our times, are we really happier than the man on the twenty-first-floor penthouse? Perhaps we are. Or perhaps it's all a myth.

But it's a nice myth to nurture. Long may it flourish!

Media baron, Ramnath Goenka, once told the editor of The Indian Express' *Sunday supplement, the poet Dom Moraes, to have a junior colleague sacked. But kind old Dom wondered how he would broach the topic. When Moraes dithered, Goenka said testily, 'I suppose you think you are too much of a gentleman. Let me tell you, gentlemen don't become rich.' Oh, for the good old middle class!*

Company for the Lonely

*If you are yearning for company,
the answer may lie within.*

Early in 2018, Britain appointed the world's first 'Minister for Loneliness'. Yes, a minister whose portfolio was to help make life bearable for those affected by social isolation. Three years later, Japan did the same. Did this help them tackle the problem? Well, it's a bit like expecting the decibel level in the local fish market to improve by appointing a union minister for polite conversation. Yet, the problem of loneliness is so widespread, and its pain so acute, that we shouldn't leave any possible remedy untried.

For years I had thought loneliness was a rich man's malaise. I doubted if the hard-slogging middle-class people, with children to be admitted to school, tax returns to be filed, gas connections to be restored and damp patches on the ceiling to be fixed, would have the leisure to reflect that they were lacking in company. But I was wrong. Experts say loneliness is income-neutral, and affects every aam admi as much as Ambani. In a global survey, around 43 per cent of Indian respondents said that they experience loneliness sometimes.

Well, social analysts who alerted the world to the 'loneliness epidemic' say the needle of suspicion points to your phone and PC. Hotshot psychologist Dr Vivek Murthy, writing in the *Harvard Business Review*, tells us that we are spending too many hours online, leaving little time for congenial eye contact, face-to-face meetings and the warmth of an arm being clasped that we are all hardwired to seek. Simply put, the more we tech, the less we touch.

Dr Murthy's theory found ready takers—probably because many among us have been fed up with technology anyway, and were looking for a good stick to whack it with. But before we avenge ourselves in a spasm of digital detox, we ought to remind ourselves that loneliness has been around for much longer than Facebook, WhatsApp, Instagram and all the rest of it. Remember the haunting lyrics in 'The Graduate'? Well, Simon & Garfunkel were 'lonely in a crowd' when social media wasn't even a gleam in a techie's eye.

In tackling loneliness, we need to acknowledge that there's no silver bullet, no single right answer. It then makes sense to adopt the modus operandi of the locksmith (your friendly neighbourhood chabiwallah). He has a bunch of keys, and so should you. One of them is sure to click.

We could start by acknowledging the problem—something most of us avoid. People who don't mind confessing even to serial bed-wetting are embarrassed to admit that they are lonely. They feel it is belittling that they are no longer part of their old circle of friends or relatives. Remember T.S. Eliot's heartless line? 'There is not a more repulsive spectacle than an old man who will not forsake the world, which has already forsaken him.'

The truth is, there's nothing to be embarrassed about. It's not your fault, or your friends' and relatives' (not even Eliot's). You sometimes run short of company for no reason other than a perverse but random chain of circumstances. Your neighbours are too busy to drop in for a chat, your sons or daughters forget to call home and your friends have problems of their own. But when you are by yourself, your imagination goes on overdrive, and you begin to see sinister patterns in people's behaviour. Relax. Speculating about people's motives is a one-way street to bitterness and despair. What you need when you are all by yourself is the patience and will to wait this phase out before a familiar, friendly face shows up at the door again.

Isolation by choice is always preferable to loneliness by compulsion. A friend of mine goes into self-imposed exile in a village in the lower Himalayas for long months every year. There's no one around to talk to for miles, and he feels miserable. But it's like an inoculation. When old age, illness or immobility does eventually deprive him of company, he will have had loads of practice.

Some people tend to fill in their lonely spells by replaying happy memories. William Wordsworth called it 'the inward eye, which is the bliss of solitude'. Well, I wouldn't know about poets because they are easily delighted and can derive happiness by thinking about anything, from daffodils to a walk in the woods. But for you and I, thinking too much of happy times gone by is entering treacherous territory. We could soon find ourselves comparing the past and present and end up feeling more miserable than before.

Instead, let's try some of the other keys from the bunch. For instance, draw up an ambitious 'To Do' list. The list could be random—learning to bake a cake, play the tabla, write a blog, nurse a money plant, etc. You may not even get halfway through your agenda, but it will ensure that you are too busy to mope around. Psychologists also advise us to immerse ourselves in things not directly linked to our own well-being. Stop thinking about your cold or cough, acne or acidity; instead, turn your focus outwards, towards issues that impact us all, and get set to fight the good fight, spiritedly saying, 'How can the banks treat us like this, how dare the municipality dig up our roads!'

Finally, if you still crave company, why outsource? Turn to the one person who is never going to go away—yourself. Your own thoughts are often more entertaining and enriching than boring company. So make sure your life is well stocked with golden memories and glorious dreams. Alternatively, you could sometimes go on what is now known as a 'self date'. On 'self dates', you dispense with accoutrements, such as girlfriends, boyfriends and any other friends, and just sit by yourself. This is not an entirely new idea. While the term 'self date' may be newly coined, the concept isn't. Over a century ago, Oscar Wilde said, 'To love oneself is the beginning of a lifelong romance.'

Happy romancing!

> 'You can cut all the flowers but you cannot keep Spring from coming.'
>
> —Pablo Neruda

The Good Thing about Gossip

It adds fizz to fellowship and serves a vital social purpose.

There's a lot of loose talk going around about gossip. The moral brigade says it injects venom into society's bloodstream, wrecks marriages, rips families asunder, turns bosom pals into backstabbers, sinks careers and sends reputations into a death spiral. That would make gossip every evil-doer's ideal—a non-violent weapon of mass destruction! True, all true. But, as profound thinkers, like the unforgettable Donald Trump, have told the world, the truth is many-sided.

So here's the alternative truth about that utterly gutterly delicious malicious tittle-tattle, which we claim we have no time for, and yet occupies a special niche in our lives.

Nattering about people who matter is, and always has been, something of a social rite of passage. It's your Aadhar Card to acceptance in the circles you covet. Take me for example. By myself, I don't have a hope in hell of making a striking impression on members of the elite groups I admire. But give me good tattle, or fun facts about people (never mind if it turns out to be more 'fun' and less 'fact'), and before you can say 'Shobhaa De' or 'Suhel Seth', I will have everybody's ear. That's how most of us are wired.

Oxford University anthropologist and social psychologist Robin Dunbar has added scientific heft to what I have just said. He claims we gossip for much the same reason that our esteemed cousins, viz., the monkeys, groom each other. They may seem to be perusing each other's person on a treasure hunt for lice, but they are actually doing something more noble and more social. They are building bonds. And that's exactly what we do too when we exchange our tangy tales.

Apart from adding fizz to fellowship, gossip is also a great leveller. Education, democracy and urban living have all been touted as tools to help place members of varying social classes on an equal footing. Well, gossip does as fine a job as democracy, etc., and with much less fuss. Just think of the kind of levelling that is achieved every afternoon when the housewife and the maid discuss the neighbour next door. Or consider the chummy camaraderie that envelops the boss and the junior executive when they get together over a beer and meticulously, if mercilessly, skin an absent senior executive.

In an ideal world, I suppose such bonding ought to happen while we talk about the graces and virtues of those not in present company. But I doubt if such a chat will gain much traction. Suppose you kick off with, 'Psst, have you heard…?' and lean into the huddle to reveal that, 'Raju volunteers as a warden for the Road Safety Patrol', or that, 'Purshottam gives free tuitions in Prakrit for the poor'. I am afraid you are going to see a precipitous drop in listenership. Speaking and hearing no evil may be a fad with the Mahatma's monkeys, but it's unlikely to keep lesser mortals engrossed.

The rise of social media has made gossip simpler to transmit than ever before. You don't need to trudge down to the village chaupal, just as our forefathers were wont to, or walk to the water cooler as today's office executives do. Technology has made it possible for us to e-gossip while slouching on the couch. But that doesn't mean crafting the story has gotten any easier. In fact, when folks say gossip is idle talk, they do the art of news trafficking an injustice. It is anything but idle.

The effective gossiper has to be on his toes 24×7. He knows that the tales he is carrying have the life expectancy of a Russian dissident. Once an event becomes public knowledge, it stops being gossip-worthy. Also, you need to know what to chat about, and when. Some subjects are clearly off the charts.

Nobody in the world gossips about mass murder, big-ticket crime or tragedies. What gets tongues wagging, ears twitching and lips smacking are those embarrassing eccentricities, the nuggets that people would prefer to kick under the carpet.

That's why we gossipers suffer very few pangs of conscience when we sit down with friends and set the ball rolling. Our motives are generally above reproach. Most of us gossip for the same reasons that Ram Gopal Varma makes movies—to entertain, divert and delight, or to use that irreplaceable Indian expression—for 'time pass'.

There is one downside to all this, of course. Whatever our motives, if you talk about others, you can bet that others will talk about you. Take it easy. Nobody gossips about a nobody. When your private affairs become fodder for hushed but animated discussions, it's a signal that you are either on your way or have already attained the big leagues.

Welcome aboard!

> 'There is no greater agony than
> bearing an untold story inside you.'
>
> —Maya Angelou

Absent-minded? Forget it.

We are only paying the price for having a poet's mind trapped in the body of a regular white collar.

Nearly six decades ago, a professor in a Walt Disney comedy bequeathed immortality to a mental failing that has been a recurring cause of red-faced embarrassment and abject apologies. The professor was bright and brainy, but so single-mindedly focused on matters of science and technology that he could never remember the more mundane 'asides' of life—including his own forthcoming wedding. *The Absent-Minded Professor* may have been a riot around the globe, but outside of filmdom and sundry works of fiction, absent-mindedness is, alas, no laughing matter.

At work, if you misplace a file, mix up meeting schedules or stand up to make the departmental presentation to the Board of Directors only to discover that your notes are in the drawer at home, you will be deemed a slacker, or feather-headed and clearly unfit for what the HR department would describe as 'higher responsibilities'. Along with other things then, you might as well forget about your next promotion.

It's the same at home too. If you've called guests over and not informed your spouse in advance, or if you go for a family vacation leaving the front door ajar or take your in-laws for a drive into the countryside having glossed over that little matter of the punctured tyre, your prospects of being called a pillar of strength for the household are as slim as Devdas being hailed as the poster-boy of family values. Lady luck is generally not on the side of the forgetful. The most important document in your file is the one you will have accidentally deleted. Phew!

Present-day society, with its fetish for practical efficiency, does not readily forgive or forget us—the serial forgetters. Word goes around that our memory has more holes than a mosquito net. The extended family will then stand on the sidelines and snigger while the spouse, out of wifely concern, suggests consulting the friendly neighbourhood neurologist, just in case all this is an early warning sign of dementia. Relax, it's nothing of the sort. Listen to the experts.

Dr George Grossberg, Director of Geriatric Psychology at St Louis University School of Medicine, says, 'Someone who misplaces their keys and gets frustrated and runs around looking for them may be absent-minded. On the other hand, the individual who misplaces their keys, doesn't know they are lost and then forgets what they are for, that's a much different level of impairment.'

If you haven't gone that far, you are in safe territory.

We of the forgetful fraternity also have historian and philosopher Yuval Noah Harari on our side. He says that the human mind is not designed to 'think like a filing cabinet'. A normal mind does not move like a regiment in a parade. Rather, like a Jasprit Bumrah run, our line of thought hops, stops and pops as memory surrenders to our poet-like imagination. Suppose your wife calls and asks you to get a packet of tea on your way home. Her words ring in your ears loud and clear as you walk towards the store, but your mind is already on its own trip. 'Tea...tea, ah, that was lousy tea the Sharmas gave us last week; and they gave us no biscuits, no chivda or snacks...those blighters are saving up I say... they must have piled up a lot of moolah by now...and on the subject of saving money, wonder how my own savings are doing...if there's any savings left that is after this lockdown... this **** government, that **** government...nobody can really do anything about a virus...' And so it goes, unlikely to ever find its way back to the cup that cheers before you reach home.

But no matter how many learned psychologists or philosophers you quote, if you are forgetful, people are still going to think you are a sap—a decent, likeable sap, but a sap nevertheless. Well, if the mountain doesn't come to Muhammad, Muhammad switches to Plan B, and so do I. My Plan B is to follow a few simple rules that will camouflage what I have forgotten.

The first rule I wrote down in my 'To Do' list is to not write anything down at all—I will forget where I kept the list in the first place. Instead, pick up your mobile and type in the list. Phones do a better job of remembering than you and I; that's why they're called smart.

Rule number two tells you how to remember names. Don't make your memory work alone—get your mouth and ears to pitch in.

Suppose I am being introduced to Manikanthan, I will ask, 'Mr Manikanthan?' (as if I hadn't heard it right the first time, and get him to repeat it). 'Ah, Ma-ni-kan-than,' I say (spacing out the syllables and relishing the phonetics). 'Hi, Manikanthan, my name is Jairam, Manikanthan.' I've heard the name four times now, and it's unlikely I am ever going to have problems on the Manikanthan front.

The third golden rule takes a leaf from Gandhiji's book. Among the Mahatma's many precepts was this: 'Everything in its place—the rubbish in its place too.' His objective, of course, was to push Indians, with our preference for litter rather than literature, towards the distant, and as yet unbranded goal, of a 'Swachh Bharat'. But we can adapt it to the problem at hand and locate things that are hiding in plain sight, like wallets, credit cards, keys, letters, ironed trousers, sunglasses… Trying to find them just before getting ready for work is like planting a sapling when you look for shade. The trick is to begin as much in advance as possible, drawing up slots for every item, and then putting 'everything in its place'. It may take some doing, but an ounce of effort is worth a kilo of comfort in crunch time.

None of these rules is bulletproof. You may master them all and still lose track of vital property documents, a winning lottery ticket and your kid's birth certificate. Well, look on the bright side. Being accepted as someone who mostly sleepwalks through life is sure to grant you general amnesty from accusations of being a 'schemer', 'opportunist' or 'manipulator'. Everyone knows you just don't have the head for it.

And finally, between you, me and this book—not everything in this big, bad world of ours is of lasting significance. Some things are best forgotten.

> 'Forgetfulness is a form of freedom.'
>
> —Kahlil Gibran

Envy-Proofing Your Life

It's easier to spot jealousy in others than in yourself.

Jealousy is one emotion that none of us will own up to. Anger, annoyance, suspicion, contempt; all are feelings we don't mind telling the world about. But jealousy? We keep it under a lid—and that's why it stews.

Since the time of the Greeks, the accepted colour of jealousy has been green (the ancient Greeks should know; even their gods went berserk with jealousy). Currently, there are fifty shades of green going around; for example, professional jealousy, rivalry between siblings, jealousy between lovers and so on. No doubt there are sound methods of envy-proofing yourself against each type of jealousy, but right now, we are going to talk largely about jealousy of the professional type.

Like Wi-Fi, jealousy's range is limited. You can hate people you have never met—terrorists, scamsters, corrupt officials, criminals you read about in the papers, even air travellers who pee recklessly. But the person you are jealous of is somebody in your proximity, likely a presumed equal, such as your colleague in the department, your neighbour or your siblings.

Heck, they are people you ought not to be harbouring nasty thoughts about in the first place!

Although it's kept under wraps, the symptoms are easy to spot. How do you know if a person is jealous of you? You apply the happiness test. Jealous people may readily sympathize with your setbacks, it is your happiness that they will not be able to countenance. So watch their reactions when you narrate some personal achievement. It could be something as minor as an invitation to a coveted musical event. Or it could be something of more significance, such as the acquiring of a new apartment in a swanky high-rise that you will be moving into.

Look at them in the eye as you are saying all this. They will, of course, mumble the usual compliments, but note if they shift uncomfortably while doing so, or if the smile seems forced (don't be fooled by the obvious turn of the lips; it's the eyes you need to focus on). Another dead giveaway is a simple remark that seems to dilute your achievement. You say that you have gotten a BMW, and he comes right back with, 'BMWs are getting quite common these days, aren't they? I saw many on the road this morning.' You can be sure the green-eyed monster has found a victim.

Umm, now let's turn to the harder part—a reality check on ourselves. This is going to be tough because we are all hardwired to spot jealousy in others much quicker than recognizing it in ourselves. Everyone's guilty to some extent—even full-time saints. As one canny philosopher said, a saint would never be jealous of you and me. But wait till he hears about the achievements of other saints!

Hard as it is, we are better off in the long run taming the monster. Jealousy is internally contagious. The way our circuitry has been laid out, we can't remain jealous of only one individual or thing. Before we know it, we become serial enviers. We begin by feeling bad about Mohan's new car, then soon are unable to stomach Mukesh's foreign trips and find ourselves seething about Monica's big break. If you are of a jealous disposition, you will always find someone or something to be jealous of.

Now, today's happiness gurus advocate the total extermination of envy. But that may be difficult, time-consuming and counterproductive. Actually, calibrated doses of jealousy do spur achievement, or as your HR Department would put it—it 'incentivizes performance'. If our forefathers didn't envy their compatriots who sallied forth into the world, we may all be still living in caves.

Science writer Norman Lobsenz said that jealousy has its roots in self-doubt or low self-esteem. For a sure-fire solution, turn to an unlikely source of strength, viz., ego. Egos have their critics, but there is no denying that ego does to envy what a hook shot does to a bouncer. It is an emphatic assertion of your own abilities. Your colleague's promotion won't upset you too much unless you begin to question your own merit. That's why it is said that no peacock is ever jealous of another one because each is sure that its tail is the prettiest in the world!

Also, we need to stop getting into the default mode of looking at all of life in comparative terms: his versus mine, theirs versus ours. That's a recipe for lifelong dissatisfaction. When your rival secures success that, in your personal opinion, is disproportionate to his merits, don't imagine that everyone and the system are conspiring against you. It's just the way life's grand lottery runs. Hang on, and wait for your number to come.

Finally, we ought not to be envious simply because it is silly. Philosopher Bertrand Russell put his finger bang on the absurdity when he said that instead of deriving pleasure from what he has, [the jealous person] derives pain from what others have. In the end, what matters is your state of mind. If you are content with yourself, what can be more enviable than that?

> 'It is not enough to succeed. Others must fail.'
>
> —Gore Vidal

Dealing with People You Don't Like

Practical tips on how to deal with the good,
the bad and the junglee.

Sometimes I can't escape the feeling that in creating this world, God scored a self-goal. They made so many rotters who do their maker no credit. But it is a bit late in the day to recall people and remodel them into the kind of men and women we like—amiable, high-spirited, straightforward, generous chaps, keen on cricket and popular cinema. This leaves us with no option but to play the cards we have been dealt, i.e., chaps who are snooty, nasty, self-centred, stingy, scheming and devious.

But help is at hand. It is a lot easier to deal with people you don't like once you are forewarned about them. So here's a conducted tour of a section of our universe's rogue's gallery. (The pronoun 'he' in the following paragraphs is for ease of reading. Be warned that the people whom you don't like and yet have to deal with can spring from any gender.)

MR MEAN

In him, the milk of human kindness has been transfused, and substituted with vinegar. Ask him for a favour, any favour—say, a lift home, or change for a hundred rupees, and he will cut you dead. Ask him his opinion about your expensive new suit, and he will damn you with faint praise. These are the chaps, as the experts tell us, who will go out of their way to deny you a benefit, even if it means they themselves suffer for it.

The field of sports has its share of meanies too, and an illuminating example is former Sri Lankan off-spinner Suraj Randiv. In a match in 2010, Virender Sehwag needed one run to complete his century, and India too needed just one to win. Randiv rose to the occasion—he overstepped the crease by a huge margin, and the resultant 'no-ball' denied Sehwag his century. There was no 'Mean Man of the Match' award, or Randiv would have won it.

Social counsellors say that the virtuous way to deal with such meanies is to forget their abysmal track record and keep expecting the best from them. I would suggest that better results may be obtained if you walk in the opposite direction. Expect the worst from them. Any time you approach Mr Mean with a request, prepare yourself to be turned down and have Plan B in place. You will then be pleasantly surprised to find out that, on some special occasions, he can even be human.

THE EGOIST

Like the chaps who lived before Galileo thought that the sun revolves around the earth, egoists believe that only they are the centre of the universe—the cherry, so to speak, in the tutti-frutti of life. So it follows that their conversation is all about 'I', 'me' and 'myself', with an occasional detour to 'ourselves' if the spouse is to be included. Frankly, nothing of what they say is spellbinding. But remember, you aren't here to curate riveting monologues. You are here to get a job done, and if the Egoist can advance your cause, your eyes should duly light up in admiration as he gives you 'Breaking News' of how he outshone his classmates at the London School of Economics/Harvard/INSEAD many years ago, or how he single-handedly outsmarted his business rivals and saved crores for the company. While you are listening avidly to all this nonsense, an 'Ooh', a 'Wah' and an occasional 'Baap re!' should escape your lips at calibrated intervals.

Do the rule books say this is flattery? Well, my book says it is 'humouring', and my book also adds that you can't make an omelette without breaking a few eggs.

Statutory warning: watch out for asymptomatic egoists. They don't display the classic symptoms; in fact, the opposite. They appear self-effacing, and they keep telling people about how humble they are, and their proud track record of always thinking of others before themselves. Don't be fooled—this is reverse snobbery in full flow. As French writer and moralist François de La Rochefoucauld said, 'Pride is never better disguised and more deceptive than when it is hidden behind the mask of humility.'

THE ARTFUL HYPOCRITE

A hypocrite is someone whose heart and lips are not, so to speak, on the same page. They say one thing but mean quite another. To some extent, let's face it, we are all hypocrites. We don't speak our minds all the time. But that's okay because the wheels of society would grind to a halt without a bit of acceptable hypocrisy, which acts as a lubricant. The kind of villains you need to watch out for are the heavy-duty hypocrites, those who are so competent at the art of double-dealing that they are not easy to spot. Since they are crafty, they usually rise to high levels in social and professional circles and are ready to backstab anyone if a knife, an opportunity and an alibi present themselves.

Eternal vigilance is the price you need to pay to deal successfully with those you have confirmed to be inveterate hypocrites. Don't discuss your plans—they will be sabotaged. Don't reveal your opinions—they could be used as evidence against you. Making the usual noises is sufficient for conversation. What does all this make you? Well, a bit of a hypocrite yourself. But then, this is permissible since you acted in self-defence.

THE ZEALOT

Zealots are alcoholics. They don't need the bottle; they are intoxicated by their beliefs. Now, the first thing that springs to mind when you hear 'zealot' is a religious fanatic. But they actually come under different labels—that of ideology, province, language and class. Whatever their label, an overdose of zeal has corroded their thought processes. So the way their mind works is elemental. If X is one of their own, well and good. If he isn't, he will be held as dirty, disloyal, clannish, stupid and petty—until it is proven that he is none of the above.

It is difficult to conduct a civil, level-headed discussion with certified zealots, and you may be tempted to play along with them to the extent possible. But watch your step, as you are entering dangerous territory. Steer clear of anything likely to set them off. Just as you work to wean an alcoholic off the bottle, you could try working towards getting the zealot to detox. You are doing a noble thing by trying to get him to be a reasonable man again. It's going to be a long haul, but you have all our good wishes.

THE KNOW-IT-ALL

He is a variant of the Egoist, described earlier. The only difference is that he is cued into the latest gossip, regularly reads the papers, watches the news channels and browses the net. Ergo, he knows it all, and so he proceeds to inform and enlighten those around him. A know-it-all does not really converse, he *pontificates*, half expecting us to take notes as they talk. Humbug of course, and it is very tempting to prick his balloon by doing a bit of prior research and showing him up to be wrong. Or you could trap him by deliberately introducing topics where you know he will be out of his depth and will start flailing desperately. The only problem with this method is that you could risk ending up as a 'Know-it-all' yourself. In the larger scheme of things, it is much better to simply nod as the Omniscient One parades his knowledge, and move on. You have better things to do than settle scores.

THE SNEAK
(or to use the more evocative Hindi equivalent, the chamcha)

Back in school, he was the teacher's pet, who went in and told her that you said '****' during recess. He no longer wears the school uniform, and his methods have gained in artfulness, but at heart he is still a rat. If a typo crops up in a mail you have written, be sure it will be gleefully borne to the boss. If you have cussed your mother-in-law behind her back, the blasphemy will definitely reach her ears. To be successful in his chosen mission of informing the authorities whenever people slip up, he needs to know what is happening. That's why sneaks inevitably end up being snoops.

Self-defence against the tribe requires a carefully worked out strategy and collaborative effort with your friends and family. You need to convey to them, gently but firmly and persistently, that the game is up and that everyone knows that they are the bearers of tales. The strategy is simple: clam up whenever they are within earshot, and say nothing that can be held against you. When silence reigns every time they come around, the message will reach home.

THE BULLY

Bullies feel a compulsive need to dominate the space they are in. Else, they fear they will perish. To deal with a bully, you need to be pragmatic. The Gujaratis are a pragmatic lot, and they have a tried and trusted way of dealing with nasty loudmouths who manspread their way across life. So an old Gujarati saying goes: 'If you are living in the jungle, make friends with the lion.'

Trying to befriend a bully doesn't mean you need to bow or scrape before him—that will make things worse. What you need to do is look for areas of engagement. You could, for instance, assist him with his tax returns or help him select an electronic gadget or give him a rare recipe for payasam. Be prepared for the long haul. The bully will not turn into a lamb overnight, but every step you take brings him closer to becoming a decent human being.

THE MISER

There are a lot of words in English to describe him, but for my money, it's the Hindi term 'kanjoos' (often clubbed with 'makhichoos') that best describes his monumental reluctance to reach for his wallet. If you want to be politically correct, you can describe him as 'price-sensitive'—the type who, when they see a rainbow, will look for the bar code.

Misers are surprisingly quick to recognize stinginess in other people, yet blind to their own shortcomings in this department. If you suggest catching the bus rather than taking a cab, they will wag their finger at you and ask you what you are saving up for. Now, having him as a friend can be a bit of a dampener for congenial companionship. But some misers continue with their extreme parsimony because they believe nobody notices it. So perhaps you will be doing him a favour by informing him that he is being called a 'kanjoos' behind his back. Even a manic miser is sensitive about his PR, and when the jokes begin to go viral, he could begin to loosen his purse strings.

This list is by no means exhaustive. There are plenty of others in this world whom you will need to learn how to deal with. I almost forgot to tell you how to deal with a bore. You know the type who will go on and on—and you have an example right here.

The solution is simple—just turn the page.

> 'To be happy, we must not be too concerned with others.'
>
> —Albert Camus

Fussing about Cussing

Of all the words in the language,
none are as useful as the four-letter ones.

GOLD MEDAL FOR GAALIS

Heard about smart cussing? It's the ability many people—including Virat Kohli and increasingly, Hardik Pandya—have developed to accurately determine just when '****' is needed, when to step up a gear and deploy '#*@* your Ω**≥!' and when the conversation needs to be kept as pure as a prayer. The guys who teach conversational skills for a living don't seem to have cottoned on to it yet, but acquiring felicity in profanity is one of the must-haves of our social and professional repertory.

We all know that there are times when nothing goes right. The sun shines, but straight into your eyes. The cuckoo calls, but its repetitiveness irritatingly sounds like your wife listing your shortcomings. The traffic is horrendous, the lights are red and the cop is mean. The boss, well...he just is. At these times, the shortest route to salvation lies in a deeply felt, forcefully articulated ****. As Mark Twain put it, 'Under certain circumstances, urgent circumstances, desperate circumstances, profanity provides a relief denied even to prayer.'

A few years ago, our film censors, umm...what do I say... Okay, bless them (mark my words, I said *bless them*), thought they would do their bit to extend Swachh Bharat into our vocabulary by outlawing 20 swear words on-screen. The drive did not last long, and the swear words regained their rightful place. This happy ending proved to the world that cussing performs as vital a function in society as the safety valve in your pressure cooker.

Apart from being a proven stress reliever, expletives lighten the atmosphere, take the stuffiness out of pompous occasions and help friends immediately strike the right wavelength. It also saves you the bother of thinking up words when your vocabulary is somewhat limited. Need an adjective, a noun, a verb or an adverb? A '****' will do the work of all! See, for instance, how your expression of appreciation rises in scale—'great', 'awesome', 'very good', 'really good'—none of these packs the punch of '****ing good'.

In the old days, girls didn't cuss. Well-brought-up girls were not even supposed to know what a swear word actually meant. There's the delightful sequence where one of Evelyn Waugh's heroines hears her fiancé (who has returned from a stint in the army) letting loose an expletive. She is incredulous and says that she thought the word was only found written in books, never spoken. And, in Arundhati Roy's *The God of Small Things*, when the matriarch berates the father of the labourer with whom her daughter is conducting a torrid affair, our eavesdropping heroine is surprised that the old lady could speak such high-voltage Malayalam.

But times have changed. In this age of gender equality, girls cannot be denied the many benefits of what is known in Hindi as 'gaali'. We have all heard of the fiery female Member of Parliament who scandalized the House with a word that had to be expunged. (I have an academic but insatiable curiosity about the epithet she used, and how many more such she knows.) To those still uninitiated, I recommend Bollywood films like *Begum Jaan* and *Lipstick Under My Burkha*. They demonstrate how the gender divide has been breached when it comes to expressing your feelings as forcefully as you want.

If you are keen to do a bit of research on the subject, you should consult Sterling Johnson's wonderfully therapeutic book, *English as a Second F*cking Language*. Vulgar language, he says, has been with us for a long time, and it can boast of a better pedigree than last year's Derby winners. He quotes

Shakespeare's Caliban (quite savage but no relative of the Taliban): 'You taught me language; and my profit on't/Is, I know how to curse.'

Arun Shourie—sometimes called the father of investigative journalism in India—should be hailed for introducing vernacular swear words into English language journalism and for making the unprintable printable. One cheery morning in March 1990, a report on the front page of *The Indian Express* said all that was not spoken in polite company. It was a verbatim account of the conversation that the then Deputy Prime Minister Devi Lal had had with Shourie. Devi Lal was livid at seeing that the morning's paper had exposed the misdeeds of his son and promptly unburdened himself of his pent-up feelings. The report was rich in invective. No beeps, no blanks and no asterisks. Shell-shocked readers saw the BCs and MCs in their pristine glory.

But the Shourie–Devi Lal episode was a single, stirring chapter in the long history of Indian journalism. Unfortunately, few Indian newspapers have continued the practice of calling a spade a spade and a '****' a '****'. As a connoisseur of cuss words, I am sorry that the precedent set by Shourie has not caught on as a trend, and am looking for more liberal climes.

You may think that in terms of cuss quotient, Punjabi is the best endowed among all Indian languages. That's probably because anything the Punjabi does, he does it with zest—even if it's casting aspersions on your sister. But all the languages in our rich and diverse land appear well stocked in the profanity department. Scholars on the subject tell us that every community and culture has its own distinctive way of swearing and that people generally tend to profane what they most value. The Chinese apparently have great respect for ancestry and genealogy. A staple abuse of an agitated Chinese, therefore, is to vow to '**** you till your eighteenth generation'. Well, now you know what to say when you meet someone from across Galwan and want to blame him for the pandemic.

Your preferred language for cussing may not always be your first language. Although my English is better than my Hindi, I feel I can express myself far better by swearing in the rashtrabhasha. In the first-class compartments of Mumbai's local trains, squabbles are common. (What else can you expect when you cram 1800 people into a compartment that seats 50!) Typically, quarrels begin in stiff, slightly stilted English as the antagonists begin to size each other up. But when both parties get into active mode, the language switches to the highly spiced vernacular.

Effective as swearing is, we need to bear in mind that like the short ball in cricket, surprise is an essential part of the impact. Binge cussing—the constant repetition of '****' can get tedious. Smart profaners, like good conversationalists, also take the extra effort to be inventive, imaginative and explicit in their use of imagery.

And finally, here's a bonus for all those who can't keep a good cuss word to themselves. A recent study has concluded that intelligent people tend to be messy, stay awake longer and…yes, swear more. So if you want to demonstrate how brilliant you are—stop fussing and start cussing.

'Never use a big word when a little filthy one will do.'

—Johnny Carson

Where There's a Bill, There's a Way

The right attitude can make paying your bills seem like a large-hearted act of philanthropy.

Parting, said a teary-eyed Juliet from the balcony, is sweet sorrow. She wasn't talking about parting with money, because for most of us, parting with hard-earned cash is much more prosaic. It is a punch in the guts and a kick in the nuts. And for harried, salaried folk, there seems to be no end to these monthly punches in the guts and kicks in the nuts. Just when we are done dealing with every bill and every EMI in sight, up springs a fresh crop of unexpected expenses: contribution to a colleague's wedding, a 'donation' for your kid's nursery building, spare parts for your air conditioner/washing machine/vintage two-wheeler, etc.

It's a natural human tendency at this stage to wish for ways to supplement your income—like moonlighting as a pakora vendor. That's not as easy as a certain prime minister makes it out to be, and as you will soon realize, it's also ineffective. Expenses are quick to gauge your new income curve and overtake earnings, and before long, it's the all too familiar punch in the gut again. A better solution to these chronic financial worries came decades ago from Champion K. and Joel Marie Teutsch. This sunny counsellor couple says that the answer to the problem lies not in our bank account but in our attitude. Yes, when we keep telling ourselves to scrimp and save—or else we will end up with a fate worse than Jet, we are creating a self-fulfilling prophecy. Instead, do the exact opposite: spend optimistically, plan boldly and make room for surpluses in your life. In short, the answer is in 'living abundantly'.

You begin living abundantly when you present your wife with a gold set instead of a silly trinket from the mall, or when you choose the more expensive tickets at the back for the Friday evening movie. If you find yourself debating about the venue for the next family dinner, choose fine dining over the fifty-rupee-thali joint down the road. Don't hesitate to walk into high-end stores with sheer glass walls that reflect a quarter of the city—the nervousness, if any, will only last for the initial minutes. See a price tag that used to be your monthly income not so long ago? Hold out before you faint. When you shuffle through multiple shirts in the 5000-rupee range, your mind will quickly acclimatize.

Also, instead of buying a single item at a time, and then quickly making your exit from the store, stand your ground and buy more—at least three shirts, more than one pair of shoes and a large crate of mangoes.

Don't worry about the stuff being wasted, and avoid getting overwhelmed by the trendy 'green' philosophy of conserving resources. Shirts are not perishable, and you are not going to wear more than one at any time anyway. When you do all of the above, and keep at it for a period of time, you raise your standard of living. This elevated lifestyle will provide you with the incentive to earn more and the capacity as well as the opportunities to do so. Equally important, it will prompt the breadwinners of tomorrow, viz., your kids, to set the bar higher for themselves.

Some of what the Teutschs have said has also been recommended by Napoleon Hill, author of *Think and Grow Rich*. This book, published nearly eighty years ago, is one of the top bestselling self-help books of all time—proving that it either works like a charm or that its readers are too shamefaced to admit they were conned. But Napoleon Hill entices you with the prospect of making a mountain of money, in the persuasive tone that reminds you of the brains behind Saradha chit funds and e-mails originating from Ethiopia. The focus of Champion Teutsch, however, is on spending rather than earning, and on freeing yourself from the grip of the middle-class mindset that prevents you from living life to the full.

Will it work? No harm in trying, and as we have been saying all along, it pays to step out of the crease sometimes. As Nietzsche said, 'What doesn't kill you, makes you stronger.' And if nothing else, you will have gifted yourself a new wardrobe!

'In spite of the cost of living, it's still popular.'

—Kathleen Norris

Know Your Bore Score

*If you tend to go on and on,
here's where you get off.*

A bore is almost always someone else. It's the neighbour who drops in for a chat and stays put until extricated from your sofa with an industry-grade suction pump. It's the babbler at a formal function who stands between you and the cocktails. Or it's the uncle whose incessant chatter and adhesive company makes you wistful about the delights of solitary confinement. Rarely does it strike us that somewhere along the course of evolution, we could have descended into prize bores ourselves.

The older we get and the higher we climb up the social or professional ladder, the more careful we need to be. Granduncles, aunts, bosses and men and women of high stature command the uncomplaining attention of their relatives and subordinates, and are unlikely to be called out and told that they are getting tedious.

So here's a 'Bore Alert', a ready reckoner that tells you that you are perhaps unwittingly but unremittingly taxing the patience of your friends.

The first step is to run a check on our ego (many bores are egoists in mufti). A pumped-up sense of self-importance prevents us from realizing that others may not be dying to learn of the celebrities we have rubbed shoulders with, the classics we have read, the exotic places we have visited, the hearts we have won and the feats of derring-do of our youth. If and when people are eager to know about our life's highlights, they will step up and say so, and we can promise them a tell-all autobiography. Until such time, it's best to keep our backstories to ourselves.

Not all bores, however, have king-size egos. I know of self-effacing men becoming champion bores because they simply don't know what to talk about. When in someone's company, the need to say something—anything—can be compelling, and the meek, therefore, make feeble attempts to fill the void with dull bits of this and that. If you are in danger of falling into this trap, step back and say nothing. Being known as the quiet sort is infinitely better than earning a reputation as a bore.

Since one man's passion is another man's poison, not everybody will find the same things boring. So it would help to gauge your audience before you engage them. Let's say you have a lot to say about Presto, your lovely little Labrador. You launch into an animated commentary about what a wonderful creature he is, how the fellow can sniff out people in the next suburb and how he springs from carpet to coffee table without upsetting the precious porcelain en route. Carried away by the momentum, you may even reveal that Presto's toilet training can be a model for millions of males in big cities—justly famed for their flair for relieving themselves al fresco. All this is spellbinding stuff, no doubt, but only for kindred dog lovers. For the rest, you are a person who is worth crossing the road to avoid.

Midway through every extended talk of yours, it pays to sensitize yourself to audience feedback. Don't wait for loud and long snores to signal that you have lost your listeners for good. Keep your eyes open for the more subtle signs, like people trying to edge away from your circle, shooting stealthy glances at the watch or those who have a distracted air like chaps who wish they were somewhere else. If any of this happens when you believe that you are at your eloquent best, you are actually running close to the danger mark.

Most bores turn out to be poor listeners and they do not respect the balanced equation—the usual give-and-take that is at the heart of a normal conversation. While you go on and on, and the sole contribution of your listeners is an occasional 'ah', 'oh-ho' and 'very nice', there's obviously so much of giving and so little of taking that it's time to bring down the curtain. Your final 'Okay, goodbye' could well be the sweetest words in the language for many.

If none of this works, there's always the clock. The legendary Krishna Menon spoke for seven hours and forty-seven minutes at the Security Council late in January 1957. He must have bored the pants off the other delegates, but he was on a mission—to deny Pakistan and its pals in the United Nations the perverse satisfaction of moving a resolution embarrassing to India on our Republic Day. Menon's marathon oratory saved the day and stymied Pakistan's attempts. Long speeches are common for many politicians. Kim Il-sung—the late 'eternal president' of North Korea—would talk to his subjects for eight hours at a stretch on topics like tractor production. But he was trying his hand at changing the mindset of his people. You and I have no such noble agendas. As they say, if we haven't struck oil in half an hour, it's time we stopped boring.

Social psychologists say that learning to be considerate of other people's feelings can shape us into better and more adjusted human beings. More to the point, we won't be called a bore.

When legendary fast bowler Wes Hall retired and became a senator of Barbados, he said, 'If you thought my run up was long, wait till you hear my speeches.'

Ageing Happily and Wisely

Life is a T20 game where the final overs can often be the most exciting.

Losing anything is tough, whether it is losing money, missing opportunities or being left out by friends. But nothing seems to trigger that aching sense of despondency as finding our youth gradually but irretrievably slipping out of our grasp. Grudgingly, we begin to agree with the saying—that life goes on long after the thrill of living. I have seen old men settling themselves on armchairs to stare misty-eyed at the world going by. They are window-shopping a youth that now appears beyond their means.

I don't think these dreary mourners are clear about what they are exactly pining for. As the Jagjit Singh ghazal goes: '*Mil jaaye to mitti hai, kho jaaye to sona hai.*' ('*If it comes our way it is mud, if we lose it, it's gold*'). Nostalgia is a seductive companion, and as we get older, we tend to believe that the past was an unending whirl of joy. Actually, that's our imagination doing a con job on our memory. It has photoshopped the times gone by, cropped unpleasant details, glossed over embarrassments and left behind a gallery of rose-tinted remembrances.

Place those same years under the scanner, and we will begin to see the cracks in the facade. We will relive the anxieties we had about our career, dredge up the petty one-upmanship of colleagues, recollect details about our plans misfiring and recall the contrived jollity of occasions where we were supposed to be having a whale of a time. That, dear reader, is the undoctored past, and coming to grips with our true yesterdays is the first step to becoming better adjusted to today and tomorrow.

Some 'senior citizens' (the term is creepy, but it fetches a bit of additional interest on fixed deposits) believe that the years post-sixty-five are an inconsequential postscript to the main segment of their lives. They are making a mistake. They don't realize that life is not a test match; it's a T20, where the final overs of the game are often the most exciting.

Here's a random list of men and women who stayed youthful into the last overs of their lives. Fauja Singh completed a marathon at ninety-three—an age when most people would consider walking around the house a feat of derring-do to be attempted only on Sundays when the family is around. Spanish mountaineer Carlos Soria Fontán summited eleven of the world's highest peaks after turning sixty. Charlie Chaplin not only kept producing path-breaking films but fathered his tenth (and not his last!) child at the age of seventy. Don Bradman led an Australian team, nicknamed 'The Invincibles', to victory at an age when today's cricketers have turned into television studio pundits. The cynics among us will carp that we can't all be Bradmans. Don't worry—the world doesn't expect you to notch up a test average of ninety-nine. If you have the zest to pick up a bat and play gully cricket with the boys, you aren't doing too badly.

I have noticed that the youthful elderly folk are almost always future-focused. Henning Holck-Larsen, legendary co-founder of the eponymous company, Larsen & Toubro, rarely looked at the rear-view mirror of his life. When asked about his early experience of nurturing a tiny partnership into an engineering and construction giant, the replies were monosyllabic. His Danish biographer says he ran into a wall completing his book, *The Tiger in His Lair*. The 'hero' appeared utterly disinterested in the past. Holck-Larsen reserved his enthusiasm instead for the firm's current performance and the prospects ahead—perhaps one of the reasons he lived to be a hearty ninety-six.

Are smartphones, digital devices and all of this much-feted digital technology making you feel like you belong to the Jurassic era? Relax, the feeling will pass, and so will the technology. Making bank transactions over the phone rather than over the counter and seeking directions from satellites rather than the local shopkeepers may appear impossible on your first try. But stay the course. You only need a little more time to go up the learning curve.

Sooner or later, everyone—at least in India—is going to be publicly and shrilly 'uncled' or 'auntied'. But neither uncle nor aunt needs to play by the stuffy rule book that our society seems to have drawn up.

Listen to that born breaker of rules, Shobhaa De. In her book, *Seventy...and to hell with it!*, the irrepressible, sexy sexagenarian offers practical tips on feeling young (as opposed to the biological impossibility of *being* young). This includes keeping abreast with the changing idioms. There's no rule that says that because you are no longer a teenager, you should only talk about profound matters in language that was used in the last century. Catch up with the latest in cricket and Bollywood. Join a club, a music circle—in fact, anything that will draw you out of the ultimate comfort zone of your home. Ms De also warns about a pitfall that old people fall into with embarrassing frequency. When asked about their health, they feel obliged to provide a conducted tour of their insides. They get eloquent about their asthma, wax lyrical about their spondylitis and narrate their death-or-glory struggles every morning on the potty. Such hardcore stuff is meant only for our doctors, or if required, for our immediate family. For all the rest, the answer to 'how are you' is simply a cheery smile.

Do we need to worry about what's going to happen to us when we get old? The answer is up to you. Life has so many moving parts that none of us can say for sure if we are going to be happy or miserable decades from today. Unless we are struck by a major reason to grieve (and tragedies could happen at any time in our lives), happiness is a matter of conscious choice. So make up your mind right now to stop eking out your years on the sidelines, and head for the dance floor.

Don't worry about what people will say. As Nietzsche put it, 'Those who were seen dancing were thought to be insane by those who could not hear the music.'

Prof. John B. Goodenough was fifty-seven when he changed our lives by co-inventing the lithium-ion battery. He went on to win the Nobel Prize in 2019. That should have been accomplishment enough for most people. In 2022, however, at ninety-four, he came up with a new ultra-efficient, low-cost version of the battery, which is set to surpass his earlier invention. After all, batteries age, life doesn't.

Yes, No...a Definite Maybe

If every coin has two sides, shouldn't you be able to see both simultaneously?

'Mirror, mirror on the wall, who is the fairest one of all?' the evil queen asked, and we all know the consequences after the mirror answered. That's one of the problems with the world today. We tend to be asked questions that sound as if they are meant to get information, but actually, the intention is to find out where our loyalties lie, and whose side we are on. I am not letting the magic mirror get off lightly in this incident either. It didn't have the elementary common sense to come up with 'er, ah… umm', and go on like the letters of the Devanagari alphabet. In other words, it hadn't learnt the value of that most useful quality in these troubled times, viz., ambivalence.

Life, as modern philosophers, thinkers and Devdutt Pattanaik assure us is not binary. There are some things that can simultaneously be right as well as wrong, attractive as well as off-putting. A reasonable mind should be able to accommodate such contradictions. Unfortunately, mankind doesn't have much of a track record for being reasonable. People compel us to take sides ('either you are with us or against us') even when we have made up our minds to not make up our minds.

Seeing you sit on the fence, some people will call you weak and indecisive. The ignoramuses don't appreciate the subtleties involved in consciously choosing to not have an opinion on every issue in the market. Also, the two things (being indecisive and accommodating contradictory opinions) are not the same. Indecisive persons are unsure and generally end up being cynical. They are the ones who will tell you the glass is half empty.

Ambivalent persons, in contrast, know exactly where they stand and why they are there. They see the glass half full, and what's more, with the right kind of fluid. They may even raise a toast to their sense of discernment. Cultivated ambivalence gives you an air of refinement. It's magisterial neutrality puts you a cut above all those who, in the heat of the moment, can't resist jumping into the fray. As the peerless Sir Humphrey Appleby says in *Yes Minister*, 'Knowledge implies complicity, ignorance has a certain dignity.'

It is not necessary for us to weigh in on every issue that comes up before us. Cricketing legend Sunil Gavaskar had said, 'Leaving a ball is sometimes more difficult than playing it.' I take the Gavaskar approach to life—it could be difficult, but it pays off in the long run. My long-standing reputation as a peacemaker and freelance conflict manager at home and office is built largely on the platform of ambivalence. After listening keenly to all that has been said, I take a deep breath. I could agree with both sides and become a populist, a crowd-pleaser. Instead, I walk in the opposite direction and disagree with both. It leaves everyone, if not equally pleased, at least equally displeased.

For all those out there, who are being pressed to take sides and want to express ambivalence in conversation, here is sound advice—literally sound. You go, 'Hmm, aah...mmm.' This could convey that you understand the situation...or it could also mean that you are clearing your throat. 'Tsk, tsk' conveys sympathy without getting into the gory details. 'Ah' and 'Oh ho' can be taken to express astonishment, but it doesn't reveal if the surprise was pleasant or otherwise. All these are the audio equivalent of modern art and are open to various interpretations. The advantage of a vocabulary with no precise meaning is that you will never be called upon to retract your earlier statement—you didn't make any in the first place. You are also unlikely to be misquoted—who would remember the exact sounds you made?

Conscientious readers may begin to wonder if they would be backing out of their responsibilities as citizens and decent human beings by seeing both sides of the coin and letting the matters rest. Hardly! Let's face it. You are not the third umpire in the world. There are, of course, some issues on which we know full well that we cannot be neutral. But those are exceptional situations. Replay the arguments you generally hear around you. Most of them are not so much about issues as they are about ego versus ego. In this war of vanities, it is best to be Switzerland.

The value of not committing oneself this way or that has been recognized at the highest quarters. Alan Greenspan, former chairman of the US Federal Reserve made it clear to the US Congress: 'Gentlemen, since I've become a central banker, I have learned to mumble with great incoherence. If I seem unduly clear to you, you must have misunderstood what I said.'

So don't let anyone hustle you. As the *WarGames* movie tells us: 'A strange game [is life]. The only winning move is not to play.'

> 'Doubt is an uncomfortable condition,
> but certainty is a ridiculous one.'
>
> —Voltaire

Killing Yourself to Stay Fit

Wanting fab abs is fine, but it doesn't make much sense to keep running for your life.

We don't need to be told about health being wealth. We've all had the phrase ringing in our ears since our first P.T. class. Then, to add more intellectual heft, along comes Arthur Schopenhauer to say, 'Health so outweighs all other blessings of life that one may truly say a healthy beggar is happier than an ailing king.' Yes, we get the message. The question is: how do you preserve this treasure? In the old days, taking care of your health was simple. If you went for the occasional waddle in the park, if your diet plan didn't revolve exclusively around pickles and fries, if you didn't smoke your heart out or get sozzled every sunset, you had more or less ticked all the boxes needed for a healthy lifestyle. Alas, not any more.

There isn't a building society in town without a clubhouse, and there's not a clubhouse without a gym, and there's not a gym…well, you get where all this is heading. It's leading to a situation where people of all ages, genders, shapes and sizes are behaving as if their lives depend on fitness (it probably does, but then man does not live by biceps alone). And while all this is going on, we hear of an increasing number of cases of young men, seemingly in excellent shape, falling victim to a heart attack.

These youths are almost certainly regulars at their respective gyms. So what happened? Dr Mukesh Goel, cardiothoracic and vascular surgeon at a leading Delhi hospital, tells us that health and fitness are entirely different, and we shouldn't confuse the two. You could achieve fitness by regularly going to the gym, but you can't get healthy there. So what happens to those who would dearly love to have a six-pack, 20-inch biceps or the politically correct 56-inch chest, but actually possess NOTA? And what happens to girls who drool over delectable outfits at a fashion store, then shake their heads and plunge into a bout of body shaming themselves?

Well, let's step back a bit, and get level-headed about our goals.

Seriously, are you (if male) aiming to get into WWF or (if female) clear the swimsuit round of Miss India pageants? If the answer is 'no', then don't let your ambition get the better of you. My ambition, for instance, is modest—it's to stave off a paunch that would herald my entry into a room a good while before I make an appearance myself. If your targets are similarly realistic, there's a world to be gained above and beyond a set of fab abs.

We all acknowledge the benefits of a session—no matter how short—at the gym. Scientists tell us that exercise is a pick-me-up for the mind. Vigorous movements increase blood flow. Oxygen-charged blood, which would otherwise have been held up in the body's Mumbai-style traffic jams, is whisked to the brain smoothly, and...eureka! You suddenly come up with solutions to problems you have been grappling with for days.

However, if you feel your brain is getting all the oxygen it can manage, consider the social aspects. Many healthy, wealthy and wise individuals have widened their circle of friends while shrinking the circle around their waists. If you want to befriend the kind of people who, well, are worth befriending, don't try meeting them at the office. Chances are you won't be able to get past the security cordon put up by the secretary and office assistant. Instead of their workplace, take a shot at the place where they work out.

An advantage here is that it is easy to think of conversation starters at the gym. Under normal circumstances, it will sound odd to spring on a casual acquaintance the question of how many sit-ups (or 'dand baithak') they do. But in the course of a morning walk, it is perfectly natural to enquire about the number of times they go round Shivaji Park. Suppose they say 'thrice', all you need to do is look adequately overawed, and you have taken the first step to building a useful relationship.

Another advantage of a strenuous workout is that it acts as a release for the day's accumulated ill temper. Dumb-bells, barbells and punching bags are ideal channels to get rid of the friction that inevitably builds up during a working day. That is probably the reason why boxers are supposed to be gentle people outside the ring as they have already released their fury while training. For the same reason, it may be a good idea to seize the initiative and proactively enrol your wife in a local health club!

If you don't feel up to pumping iron or jogging across the suburb every morning, you now have an officially sponsored alternative, viz., yoga. This ancient discipline is now enjoying a bull run. Yoga is not as competitive as practically everything else these days—no duel on the mat, no World Cup Yoga finals to trigger an anxiety syndrome. You choose pace and posture and hold an asana only as long as you are able to. It's not mandatory to sling your leg around your neck or tie yourself into a reef knot (that's Baba Ramdev territory). And if all you want to do is lie down and play dead, there's always Shavasana!

So take your pick. Surya Namaskara, pilates, aerobics, weight training or dand baithak. There's a lot on offer. As soon as you finish reading this book, how about picking up those dumb-bells?

> 'Yoga is a way of getting totally drunk [...] on life.
> They call it divine.'
>
> —Sadhguru

Cooking Up Corporate Statements

What's a journey without a destination, and what's corporate life without a statement of purpose?

You don't need to be a student of history to know that man has achieved a lot since he's been around. He invented the wheel and got the Industrial Revolution going so that machines could do most of the grunt work; he discovered useful things like penicillin, piña colada and the PC, learnt to unsling rockets and reverse swing, put men on the moon—and all of it without the aid of a 'vision statement', or its fraternal twin, the 'mission statement'.

But somewhere along the way, between subduing the Huns and the rise of ISIS, came the management consultants. After overrunning large parts of the corporate world, these formidable tribes took a long, hard look at humanity's track record and shook their heads in grave disapproval. Humanity could have done a lot more, a lot faster, they said, if only the tool of a vision/mission statement had been available.

And so, it has come to pass that a statement of purpose and a 'reason for being' is to corporates what the Aadhar Card is for you and me. We don't seem to find any real use for it, but not having one handy could prove embarrassing—especially if your job involves dealing with management consultants on a regular basis. Telling a McKinsey executive you don't give a hoot for the corporate statement is like a rookie commie telling Chairman Mao that he can't be bothered with *The Little Red Book* and has, in fact, made paper boats with its pages.

Companies pay obeisance to their corporate bible in wondrous ways. Some have got the statements framed and prominently displayed in the boardroom and all points south where employees assemble, including conference rooms, canteens, the underground parking lot and the executive loo. You could also publish it on the first page of your corporate brochure. If you really want to score big, print them in little laminated cards and ask your employees to carry them around in their trouser pockets. The consultants will love you for this.

Before the statements are mass-printed, however, they need to be written. Actually, it's pretty easy to write if you have been good at English composition in school. Left to yourself, you could probably turn out a couple of serviceable statements on any given afternoon. But as KPMG would tell you, that's not kosher.

Like sex, creating a vision/mission statement the right way means that it must not be done alone. It is supposed to embody the collective goals of the entire team and articulate, in immaculate prose, the innermost sentiments of a multitude. The call, therefore, goes out from the president's office, asking departmental heads to provide inputs. Since it's the president who is asking, contributions flow in thick and fast, with many of the more evocative lines lifted unabashedly from British and American companies. Then, if you happen to be in corporate communications, it's up to you to fit faux sentiment, raucous rants and cringeworthy profundities into a cogent whole.

That brings me to the main point of this piece, viz., a DIY guide on preparing vision/mission statements good enough to eat. Like your colleagues did all of last week, you too could start by looking at the successful efforts of other companies. Run through a handful of them (as we all know, looking at one statement betrays intent to plagiarize; looking at a dozen is praiseworthy and promotion-worthy research).

Recipe: Take a fistful of the polysyllabic nouns you have culled, such as 'cross-functional commitment', 'value bedrock', 'future-centric' and 'empowering environment'. Whisk the mix as if your life depended on it (your next promotion certainly does). Into the pot now goes common management jargon—it's the dal in the corporate khichdi of statements. Sauté with generous dollops of 'zeal', 'passion', 'aspirations' and 'learnings'. If you are feeling adventurous, lightly sprinkle 'empathy'. Organizations, where patriotism runs high, can opt for an Indian tadka. They toss in 'close alignment with national priorities' and 'dovetailing corporate objectives with the country's interests'. Your local MP and MLA will like it if you add 'aatmanirbharta' because it could be the only word they have previously come across.

You may find all this a bit hard to stomach but lay it on thick anyway. Vision statements were never meant for the delicately nurtured.

Done? Not quite. No corporate statement is complete without a dressing of concern for climate/community/diversity and inclusion/the disadvantaged, and at a stretch, even the LGBT community. So a 'social and environmental conscience' is the cherry you add after you have placed your masterpiece on a platter.

Voila! A vision statement as good as McKinsey's mother made.

'Because we all eat lies when our hearts are hungry.'

—Penelope Douglas

Fool is Cool

Have you put your foot in your mouth any time lately? Or been caught with your pants down? Relax. Professional help is at hand.

A recurring cause of stress in our times is the fear of doing something stupid or saying the wrong thing. Society is prickly in its own way, and it expects us to be relentlessly reasonable, uniformly mature and 'politically correct' 24×7. Yes, we all know that man is a rational animal—but sometimes even reason needs to take the afternoon off, or as we say in Mumbai's inimitable lexicon, do a 'dandi'.

A century ago, American writer and philosopher Elbert Hubbard had said, 'Every man is a damn fool for at least five minutes every day; wisdom consists in not exceeding the limit.' Perhaps Hubbard was prescient (maybe he knew that one day they would have a leader called Donald Trump). I think he was also on to something profound, and his theory deserves wider recognition. Yes, it's time all of us insisted on our five-minute allowance and turned it into a universal human right. We should be allowed to exercise our right to be a 'damn fool' anytime, whether when we are caught off guard (which happens all the time with me), when we are inebriated (which, hic, happens even more often) or when we bravely step outside our field of expertise. The last mishap, for instance, is common with Bollywood stars. Put a script in their hands and they will morph expertly into an ardent lover, bristling cop, cackling villain or deep-voiced do-gooder. But bereft of a script and minus a director guiding their every move, they can only be themselves, and that's when the fool gets free rein.

Take Salman Khan. He is an honourable man with a six-pack. Ask him to talk about the stuff that is regularly featured on 'Page 3' and he will fill up the colour supplements all by himself. But ask him about social issues, political issues, economic issues, in fact, pretty much anything outside the colour supplements, and you are skating on thin ice. So it is with almost every other denizen of tinsel town: Shah Rukh

Khan, Anupam Kher, the late Om Puri (after sunset), Aamir Khan and even the immensely gifted but mercurial Naseeruddin Shah. All of them are decent, level-headed gentlemen, yet each of them has at one time or another slipped on the banana peel of social acceptability. They usually don't step over the line for more than a few minutes, but it's enough time for national outrage to boil over from tweets to the streets.

Outside of Bollywood, the list of those who sorely need their 'damn fool' time is long and growing. Let's take our netas. Five minutes is clearly inadequate. When in full flow, and if unchecked by those around them, our netas can be a constant source of embarrassment even for their most ardent bhakts. During the coronavirus pandemic, our fears and anxieties were often punctuated with hilarity as political leaders stepped onstage to offer a clutch of miracle cures backed by staggeringly scientific explanations. Then we have yoga gurus who contort themselves only to put their foot inextricably into their mouths, cricketers who make a 'silly point' and retired soldiers who shoot themselves in the foot and (how can we forget) TV anchors who believe that absurdity will become acceptable if spoken in a loud enough voice.

Don't be under the impression that it is only in these stressful modern times that people in the public eye have begun to say stupid things. Actually, wise men and women could have been guilty of talking nonsense for ages, but the word just never got around. I am sure if Socrates, Confucius or our very own Chanakya had made a prize gaffe, his disciples would glance at each other, smile…and pretend it was never said. But today's round-the-clock media scrutiny leaves no room for such discretion. Your misstep is frozen in the frame for prime time, transmitted across the world and soon acquires a life of its own on social media.

Constant media coverage also has other fallouts. When a topic—any topic—is discussed threadbare by panels of resident and roving experts on a hundred-odd TV channels, the point of saturation is quickly reached. Beyond that, even the keenest mind and the sharpest intellect will find it hard to spot fresh angles or contribute any meaningful perspectives. A foolish comment, then, is the consequence of all the intelligent positions being already taken.

In such circumstances, the best thing to do when a mike bearing the logo of a leading news channel is thrust at you is to step back and say, 'I pass'. But it's hard to let go of the opportunity of the few minutes of fame, and even the strong-willed succumb. Their ill-fated attempts at profundity are the stuff of derisory headlines the next day, and these kickstart protests on social media that can linger for weeks.

Now, let's look around us in our immediate circle. All that was said above is also true of our friends and acquaintances. By holding the people we deal with accountable for everything they say or do, and expecting them to consistently meet a lofty standard of speech and action, we prevent them from being their true, spontaneous selves. They (and we) are flawed and will never be perfect beings. We are human beings.

So let's give our friends, colleagues, uncles, aunts and neighbours a priceless, spiritually liberating gift: Go ahead guys, you don't need to look over your shoulder all the time. Being somewhat stupid some of the time won't be held against you.

Fool is cool.

> 'Everyone is born a genius, but the process of living de-geniuses them.'
>
> —Buckminster Fuller

Touch Wood, Chashmebaddoor!

Because very little in life seems to be making sense,
it's smart to bet on nonsense.

Superstition is having a run of bad luck. Debunked by the straight and narrow thinkers, shamed by science, and called sexist names like 'old wife's tales', you would have thought that nobody would have the slightest qualms about setting off for a journey on Friday the 13th, breaking a mirror, getting cursed by transgender folk, spilling salt after sunset or letting a black cat cross your path any more. Well actually, we would rather have none of the above happen, because while superstition may be down, it's not out. Like infiltrators through a porous border, the freakiest of beliefs have stolen in and lodged themselves inextricably in our systems.

That's why we all have our lucky shirts, our lucky numbers and our good luck charms. Like the Pepsi of old, there is nothing official about it. Officially, we do not believe in all this bunkum. But I still won't whistle after sunset because my aunt in Taliparamba had convinced me that it attracts snakes into the house. Science tells me that snakes are deaf, and even if they aren't, they would hear precious little above the late-evening Mumbai traffic. But why take the risk?

It's not just you and I who are adopting this safety-first approach. Sportsmen do it too, and so do filmmakers, writers and celebs of all stripes. Ernest Hemingway, for instance, would never talk about the book that he would write next for fear that it would spook its chances of success. And funnily enough, the very chaps who giggle and snigger when grandma takes elaborate preventive action to evade the baleful influence of an eclipse will watch with silent awe and even a touch of reverence when Sachin, Rohit or Virat go about their equally elaborate and equally weird pre-match rituals.

One reason, of course, is that laughing at Virat Kohli can be injurious to health. But there's another reason. Cricketers say it helps them get into their 'zone' and perform better, and who will argue with a string of victories—give or take a World Cup? Psychologists, too, have given a 'thumbs up' to this method of getting set for a marquee moment. Any set of repetitive, although seemingly meaningless, actions (a.k.a. rituals) that generate self-belief has a calming effect on the nerves and can lead to a spike in performance.

On the flip side, superstition also softens the blows that life dishes out now and again. When French playwright and novelist Jean Cocteau was asked if he believed in luck, he replied, 'We must believe in luck. For how else can we explain the success of those we don't like?' I have observed that when it is time for a promotion or an increment, the goddess of fortune unfailingly skips me and smiles instead at that overrated, over-paid fool in the next cubicle. I am not surprised for I know the real reason. His cabin is facing north by north-east (on the preferred route of positive energies) and mine is, well, facing the staff toilet. When my grand-uncle, grand-aunt and not-so-grand I set off to resolve a long-pending family dispute and failed resoundingly in our efforts, I know where the fault lies. It all happened because we were three. Silly me, I had forgotten the wise old saying: 'Teen tigada kaam bigada.' (Any group of three brings ill luck.)

Superstition adds a delightful tangent to the drab and linear cause-and-effect relationships that logic bhakts tout. Little girls are told not to snatch at coconut shavings while it is being grated. Not because they could hurt themselves on the sharp-toothed grater, but because of a more long-term and dire consequence: it is sure to rain on their wedding day! And when my right eye twitches, science tells me that it's due to an excess of caffeine. But I prefer to think it signals money coming my way.

Life is a lottery, or rather, a series of lotteries, with multiple draws. How you fare, whom you meet, how your children shape up and how happy you finally get to be—it all depends on so many variables that you are unlikely to find any logical link to connect them all. It's best to keep the amulet and talisman handy. Danish physicist and Nobel Prize winner Niels Bohr is reported to have had a horseshoe nailed to his door. When asked if a man of science like him actually believed in superstition, he said, 'No, but I am told it works even if you don't believe in it.'

Of course, giving the supernatural total control over your life would be stupid. Instead, the smart thing to do is to meet superstition halfway and opt for a diet version that won't disturb the peace, cause bodily harm, come in the way of our neighbours, hurt the environment or cost too much money. To paraphrase P.G. Wodehouse, while we don't have to be superstitious, we can jolly well be 'stitious'!

'When an ancient Roman stumbled on the threshold as he left the house, he gave up his plans for the day. This seems to us senseless, but under primitive conditions of life such an omen inclines one at least to be cautious.'

—Carl Jung

No Sin Being Cynics

You can't be let down
if you were not up in the first place.

Cynics are easy to spot. They are the ones who pull the plug on general optimism and warn of hard times saying, 'The worst is still to come.' Even as they are opening a gift wrapping, they tell everyone around that the shiny little object under all those layers of bubble wrap is going to be something silly. As for the time-honoured, character-defining question about the glass, their response would be—it's half-empty, and what's worse, what's left in the glass is unfit for human consumption.

Given these off-centre views, cynics are not cut out to win sundry popularity contests. Optimists can't stand them because they refuse to look at life through rose-tinted spectacles. Politicians hate them for they will never constitute those drops that make up a 'wave' at election time. As for the general public, it has been schooled into believing that listening to cynics will somehow make those dire predictions come true.

How do I know all this? Because I'm a card-carrying cynic myself, and I believe it's time we votaries of worst-case scenarios did a bit of image-building for ourselves. Look at our track record. We disbelieved the stuff we read in the newspapers decades before fake news became an industry standard. We complained that summer afternoons were getting warmer way back when Greta Thunberg was only the proverbial gleam in her father's eye. We dismissed the US presidency as a joke long before Trump put in an appearance. And what do we get for all this remarkable prescience? We get to be called bad news, wet blankets, party-poopers…the term for it in Hindi hits harder, 'panvati'.

The fact is that the world is too trusting for its own good. Far from the 'trust deficit' that everyone seems to be talking about, what society suffers from most is a trust surfeit—a gullibility glut, with unwary (and, *ahem*, un-cynical) people ready to get off the mark and spout passwords, PINs and OTPs to anyone who comes along with a get-rich-quick scheme. If only they had consulted the watchdogs of society's well-being (us naysayers), we would have told them that the schemes are appropriately named. It's only the schemers who get rich quickly.

Now, when acting as watchdogs, you are going to bark a bit and act like a stern schoolmaster. (What's the use of a watchdog that can only wag its tail?) You may often chance upon cynics who are grumpy. Still, it's a mistake to think that the frown is the default expression of the cynic. Take me for instance. The sunny smile I wear at most times is as wide as my social media profile picture. And there's good reason for this genial disposition. When you expect the worst, you are pleasantly surprised by what actually happens. Quite simply, you can't be let down when you are not up in the first place.

Here's what we do best: we are responsible account holders because we never believe what banks say on their websites. When a happiness guru comes along and recommends a mantra that will dispel everything, from heartache to toothache, we treat him the way you treat an e-mail from Ethiopia promising a bonanza; and when someone offers a wonder drug that will give you the complexion of Alia Bhatt and the wisdom of Aryabhatta, turn your grey hair into jet black and reduce weight in your sleep, we dismiss them with the same sceptical look that our forefathers did to the men who promised to turn copper into gold.

Most of all, cynics make model parents. We do not saddle our children with outsized expectations, such as taking over as CEO of a global tech company or goading them to win a Nobel. I got my cynical gene from my dad—justly famed as the Perennial Pessimist of Puthiyedath. Modest in his expectations, he never banked on either of his sons setting Mumbai's seasonal river, the Mithi, on fire. In fact, sizing up my intellect and aptitude accurately, he gauged that I was good enough to be appointed as a higher division clerk in the city's municipal corporation (anything above that was a bonus).

It was a life lesson that has stood me in good stead in everything I do, including writing this book. After I mailed it to the editors, I told myself that it was sure to end up in the recycle bin alongside a million other attempts, and forgot all about it.

Then…oh, what a pleasant surprise!

> 'Never let success hide its emptiness from you, achievement its nothingness, toil its desolation.'
>
> —Dag Hammarskjold

Flying High in Borrowed Feathers

To clinch arguments or appear knowledgeable,
borrowed wisdom is your best ally.

Social media has kicked off a new, high-growth ancillary industry. It centres around borrowed wisdom and expresses itself in quotations. Incessantly through the day and night, my mobile blinks as decorated generals advise me on how to battle the problems of life, respected industrialists reveal the secret sauce of their success and former cricketers prop up my morale by telling me that the match is not lost till the last ball is bowled. I doubt if this incessant exposure to great sayings has improved me as a person, but it has convinced me of the persuasive power of quotation marks.

The quotation mark is literally a cut above the run-of-the-mill punctuation. In its previous life, I am sure it was just a comma—one of the scores strewn across the text, with nobody, except grammar Nazis, giving it a second glance. But inverted, elevated and paired with its twin, it confers gravitas to content. Epigrams become wittier because you know they are by Oscar Wilde, observations acquire depth and heft as they now have Einstein's name appended to them, and when someone like Mother Teresa tells you how to turn compassion into action, who are you to argue?

To be honest, not all the things you read within those parenthetical commas are of particularly high voltage. As you sometimes react when you see perplexing examples of modern art, you feel you could have come up with similar stuff yourself. Alas, in the status-conscious, nomenclature-enamoured world we live in, what is said matters less than who said it. So unless your name happens to be Ralph Waldo Emerson, Rabindranath Tagore or Confucius, your thoughts will find few takers.

I believe man's respect for the quotation mark flows out of our deference to authority. As kids, the authority is vested with our parents or school teachers. 'Daddy had said' or 'teacher won't like it' was enough to end a debate. Alas, we no longer live in a world where a single opinion is decisive on all matters. But look at the bright side—the explosion of 'authorities' gives you a larger arsenal to choose from when you are heatedly arguing a point and looking to deploy heavy artillery. Apart from helping you score points off a friend, family or foe, quotations can work wonders for your brand. Suppose you are trying to lift everyone's mood in these uncertain times. Instead of the conventional *'hum honge kaamyab'* ('we will succeed') you enlist Tagore saying, 'Faith is the bird that feels the light and sings when the dawn is still dark.' Imagine that! You are quoting Tagore as easily as you would hum a hit number. Your brand value will touch the ceiling.

Modern technology has made the quest for quotes easy— just key in the appropriate word, and the genie of search engines will do the rest. If luck favours you, you will locate a line that speaks your mind in a memorable fashion. If that doesn't work, you will need to make your own luck. In other words, necessity will make you the mother, not just of invention, but of a quotation. If you are the conservative sort who sticks to the rules as far as possible, you can simply tweak an existing line till it meets your exact needs. However, if you are not averse to stepping out of the line and ready to swing your bat like Suryakumar Yadav, you can try your hand at DIY quotations. Simply write something that has a twist, a punch or a sting in its tale, and then ascribe it to somebody well-known, wise and worthy. A word of advice from a veteran counterfeiter of quotations: avoid the usual suspects and pick a tier-two intellectual. Almost everyone would have heard of him, but few would be able to recollect all his writings.

Don't be overly bothered about the scruples of putting your own spin on history. Social media is brimming with what could be called the illegitimate offspring of intellectuals. You also have the venerable Voltaire on your side; 'what is history', the French thinker had said, 'but a fable agreed upon!' For the record, this quotation *itself* is a matter of dispute. Was it by Voltaire, Napoleon, Bovier de Fontenelle or Emerson? Nobody is certain, and frankly, not many are bothered. All it proves is that what really matters is neither the creator nor the content, but the quotation mark.

Talking of counterfeit quotes and not talking of Bob Dylan is like conversing about Covid and not mentioning Wuhan. While critics have surfaced off and on, pointing out that some of Dylan's lines are borrowed, it was in the acceptance speech for the Nobel Prize for Literature (worth all of ten million Swedish Kronor plus a gold medal), that the iconic singer stepped up a gear. He told the world that he had been inspired by the American classic Moby Dick. To show just how much he was moved by the famed tale of the whale, Dylan quoted a line from Herman Melville's book. There the matter would have rested had an indefatigable evangelist of truth (such people exist) not pointed out that the lines Dylan had quoted appeared nowhere in the original book but were, in fact, taken from a school guidebook. Obviously, when facing the daunting prospect of ploughing through the complex and sometimes turgid Moby Dick (all 377 pages of it), Dylan did what every sensible schoolboy would do—he took a convenient shortcut and consulted a guidebook. Well, when you and I did it in school, we were told off. When Bob Dylan does it, he gets a Nobel Prize. That's life, guys!

Facing a 'Firing'

What to do when the guns begin to boom?

Indians have contributed a fistful of gems to the treasure chest of English vocabulary. For my money, the best of the lot is the ominously onomatopoeic 'firing' used as we Indians do, to describe verbal heavy artillery. Think of the sound effects it brings to mind: 'You ingenious idiot! Boom! Blam! You freakish fool! Kaboom! Aargh! You sublime scoundrel! Dishoom!' Think of gore and more being spilt. Now, spend another minute comparing this word with its starchy synonyms, like 'admonish', 'censure', 'reprimand', 'reproach', 'scold', etc. How typically Enid Blyton-ish; how utterly insipid! Well, you can occupy your mind with all this when you actually are at the receiving end of a firing. It helps cushion the blows.

In an ideal world, nobody should need to give anyone else a tongue-lashing. But we do not, as you would have gathered by now, live in an ideal world. In the combustible environment we inhabit, tempers can erupt for reasons good and bad. The bosses could deem that the contemptuous expression you put on every time they are speaking is a breach of office decorum. Or the uncle whose carefully cultivated reputation you have (to borrow an evocative expression from Hindi) made a 'falooda' of, may turn nasty. Or sometimes, the avalanche hurtles down for no reason at all. I, for instance, am frequently hauled over the coals simply because coals are available, and there I am, eminently haulable.

With my first-hand experience in reporting from ground zero and having been at the receiving end, I can tell you that the world is made of two kinds of people—those who go in for bouncers and those who opt for spinners. Pace bowlers are bawlers. At full throttle, their voice can scale up to 110 decibels, which is not much below the roar of the K9 howitzer acquired by the Indian Army. Spinners, in contrast, let their choice of words do the damage rather than relying on their volume. Carefully chosen, with silken but stinging references to your family background and credentials, they induce in you a profound and sometimes permanent sense of worthlessness.

Whether you are facing a fast bowler or a spinner, wise counsellors will advise you to quietly accept all that comes your way. But I boldly walk in the opposite direction. I am for giving it right back. The only thing is that I take the precaution of muting all my responses. This is how the scene then pans out (words in brackets are played out in my mind):

Boss: 'Nonsense, nonsense, NONSENSE! All I hear from you all day is nonsense. Really, I need no more of your nonsense.'

(Sir, I think what you do need is a thesaurus.)

Department head: 'The whole office is subpar. There's an idiot in stores, another in strategy, a half-wit in finance, an imbecile in IT, and there you stand—the star of the show.'

(At least our HR policy is consistent.)

In a domestic situation, it could be spoken by your enraged uncle. 'You come from a long lineage of losers. Go back up your family tree, and you will find that none of your family has ever been up to much.'

(How far up the tree should I go, uncle—right back to the monkeys from whom both you and I have descended?)

When the guns begin to boom, the people around you— your neighbours at home and colleagues in the office—may pretend not to notice. This is good-natured PR. Make no mistake, they are paying attention to every word and filing it away for future reference—if and when required. But don't let this disturb you. As Aristotle said, 'man is by nature a social animal', and animals are sometimes solicitous and always inquisitive. What's more, nobody is going to think less of you because you've got a mouthful. Remember good old Michelangelo? He was frequently chided by his wealthy patrons. But their incessant sniping did nothing to diminish the artist's stature. If anything, it made his artistic achievements seem heroic.

Rather than bothering about other people's reactions, focus instead on your own body language. One school of thought suggests that you put your chin up and look the firing squad straight in the eye. That's a brave decision to take, but it is fraught with risks. Rajat Gupta—ill-starred head of McKinsey and Goldman Sachs—tells us in *Mind Without Fear* that he refused to look sufficiently submissive when the jail warden turned his eyes on him. Gupta had to pay a high price for the lack of conspicuous distress. Another school says that you will be let off lightly if you have an 'apology' written large on your face. Between these two extremes lies the most wicked and wily way of expressing resentment of authority; you must do what the Ethiopians do. A saying from the ancient fields of Ethiopia goes: 'When the great lord passes, the wise peasant bows deeply and silently farts.'

Well, nothing lasts forever.

Time passes, bahu becomes saas, junior becomes boss and the tables are turned. You are now, or will soon be, in the exalted status of a person entitled to give rather than get a firing. When you choose to dish it out, remember the rules you learnt long ago—and don't take your junior's submission at face value. Well, if push comes to shove, and you have to play your last card, turn to the other word that we Indians have contributed to the English language in addition to 'firing'.

It's 'aiyyo!'

> 'Everyone behaves badly—given the chance.'
>
> —Ernest Hemingway

Worrying Works Wonders

Never mind what motivational speakers and all-weather optimists say—worrying is good for you.

This seems to be an era of stress. We are worried about falling ill, getting fat, going bald, growing old, losing money, getting sacked, being snubbed, feeling lonely… We mope about opportunities missed and what might have been. Worst of all, we worry that we spend so much time worrying.

The truth is that man is a natural-born worrier. We would have continued the way God made us if Dale Carnegie hadn't come along. This high-octane salesman turned writer, with a flair for the good story, spooked society with the insidious theory that we aren't living right unless we have smiled every last anxiety out of sight. He must have known which button to press because millions of gullible readers across the world, all of whom had been getting on with their lives without undue fuss, suddenly began to worry about worrying.

The baton has since been passed down to a gaggle of happiness gurus and pop philosophers who pontificate in accents redolent of strong South Indian coffee. Together they have turned a perfectly natural mental state into Public Enemy Number One. So how does one win the war over worrying? Simple—you beat the enemy by joining him. Yes, a growing body of research is now showing us that we worriers actually have a good thing going for us.

Listen to the experts: 'Worrying is the evolutionary by-product of advanced intelligence.' Insects don't worry, and neither do animals or imbeciles. It's only wise folks like you and I who do—QED. As an accomplished worrier, I have never cared for those in the opposite camp who have let themselves be swayed by all that talk about the perils of worrying. Actually, full-frontal worrying is the sincerest expression of concern.

Imagine a Category 5 storm brewing in your family. Your venerable aunt has just published a book of poems in which she poured out her poignant soul. Alas, the book has met with the kind of cordiality a 'Me Too' accused can expect from the militant wing of the Mahila Sangh. The poem's lines have been lampooned, its rhymes rubbished, its metre mauled and its flights of fancy...well, you don't want me to go that way.

This is when the ace worrier in me rises to the occasion. I let the furrows on my forehead advertise how deeply the news has affected me. Sometimes I even step up a gear, i.e., ask for a glass of water, and crash into the nearest divan, clutching my head in my hands. The elders are quick to notice. '*Mon* (that's me) has taken the news badly,' they say, sympathizing with my sensitive side. 'Not like those other fellows who don't give a damn about poor Ammalu amma.'

At this stage, protocol demands that loyal relatives swing into damage control mode by taking to social media by tackling trolls and seeking professional counsel from everyone in sight—from top-flight PR agencies to panwallahs. But given my frazzled state, I am exempted from such duties, and the same is duly delegated to those better suited to discharge them. Honestly, you won't come across a more effective labour-saving device than worrying.

I feel the reason that the world's in such a mess today is because fools are rushing in where we worriers fear to tread. They take to the streets, or to tweets, and before you know it, the situation has turned ugly. If only they had the sense to step back, sit down (as directed above) and worry until temperatures returned to normal!

Worrying is also your best bet against boredom because you obviously can't be anxious and bored at the same time.

Now, conventional wisdom may tell you the right way to relieve the tedium of a slow Sunday afternoon is to take up a hobby. Well, you can tell conventional wisdom to take a walk. There's only so much of Sudoku or hu tu tu, crocheting or kayaking, origami or bigamy that a man or woman can do. Much better to take up worrying.

Recent studies by blameless people of considerable repute have found that people who worry have less of a protein known as galectin-3, which is commonly associated with the conditions that cause heart disease, strokes and diabetes. This means that apart from all the benefits mentioned, worrying can also reduce your medical expenses.

So I recommend that as soon as you finish reading this book, you draw up a 'To Worry' list. After you have worried your way through all the items, you can upgrade from personal issues to international matters. Take up pandemics (their likely cause and sure-fire cure), rising intolerance, falling academic standards, widening economic disparities and the chances of World War III breaking out before you can get to the ATM.

Ah, oodles to worry about!

> 'I am a chronic worrier.'
>
> —Kate Sweeney

The Tyranny of Thought

Like overeating, over-exertion and overdoing anything, overthinking is also injurious to health.

Seven decades ago, we won freedom from those who had colonized our land. It's time now to free ourselves from an insidious practice, which has, for all practical purposes, colonized our minds, viz., the tendency to think too often, too hard and too long. Worse, we even begin to believe that we have done our good deed for the day by putting in long hours of uninterrupted thought.

It's easy to figure out how it all began.

Back in the day, when we were evolving from apes, our great-grand-ancestors must have realized that their puny muscles were no match for those he shared the jungle with—lions, elephants and the mastodon. They weren't fleet of foot, didn't possess venomous fangs or even a decent shell to huddle under when things got rough. So it must have crossed their mind that he scored above the competition in the thinking department. The advertising consultant from the cave next door would have agreed heartily, and come up with a pithy profundity, typical of his tribe, and told them the ability to think is 'humankind's USP'. Our forefather then drew the most logical conclusion: the more I think, the better my chances of not becoming the sabre-toothed tiger's snack.

What began purely as a self-defence mechanism seems to have ended up becoming the main business of our lives—and the world right now has too many thinkers for its own good. These thinking classes do not seem to have noticed that the world has changed. The tigers are in zoos, the mastodons are in the pages of zoology books and the elephant gives rides to children when he is not starring in *National Geographic* films.

There is really no need to think so much anymore. But we have fallen into the habit, and we all know how difficult it is to break a bad habit. To make matters worse, we have had philosophers like Descartes adding fuel to the cerebral fire with such pronouncements as 'I think, therefore I am'. This was music to the thinker's ears, and it gave thinking pride of place over what ought to be more natural human activities, like watching gorgeous sunsets, , gossiping, playing the fool and figuring out how to get yourself a cup of tea. Look at yourself in the mirror. We are thinking all the time, over-analysing what has been said or done. What did the boss mean when he told me that I would not be needed for the next meeting? Am I going to be eased out in this crunch situation? Or what were Pandurang and Padmaja saying when I spotted them in the corridor? Were they, by any chance, talking about me? (And come to think of it, what were they doing together in the first place?) When my in-laws smile why does it look as if their hearts are not in it? Why...and so it goes on.

Like the junk that tends to accumulate in the loft, much of what we think about is actually meant for disposal. So summon your mental raddiwallah and tell him to take the lot. While you are at it, direct him to a few of your neighbours—workaholics whose mental horizon is limited to their workplace; religious fanatics of every hue who think too much about their faith; and don't forget the self-centred lot who think only about themselves all the time.

Many of us mistakenly believe that the problems we are confronted with can be solved by the power of concentrated thought and that such a tour de force of thinking will put us on the road to lasting happiness. How naïve can you be! American novelist Jonathan Safran Foer spoke for all of us in the opposite camp when he said: 'I think and think and think, I've thought myself out of happiness one million times, but never once into it.' Do I hear you saying that you have important issues you need to wrestle with? Who doesn't? But most demons in our mind are self-created and can therefore be self-neutralized. As for the problems that persist, perhaps you should learn the art of peaceful coexistence.

If you don't believe me, consult your friendly neighbourhood gurus. Their first advice would be to reduce the burden of thought. I did not meet a spiritual guru early enough, but I had my father as counsel. He took life as it came, did not bother much about cause or consequence and spent a largely carefree and blameless life. The first day he ever spent in hospital was his last.

I am not suggesting that we bid goodbye forever to thinking. That would be dangerously stupid. Instead, apply the golden principle of moderation. Think whenever it is necessary, and then hold yourself back before your thoughts sow the seeds of worries that will soon grow into the poison ivy of anxiety. Let's face it, no amount of anticipatory thinking will help you understand the workings of fate or solve the problems that may crop up in the future. As wise people before me, have said, let's not allow our today to be held hostage to either yesterday or tomorrow.

If we want our children to lead lives happier than ours, I think we need to teach them the importance of un-thinking. Tell them not to exercise that part of the mind for more than is strictly necessary. Anything above the bare minimum produces diminishing returns and disturbs your peace of mind.

What I am proposing is rather unconventional, and you may want to think it over. Oops, think? See, I haven't got rid of the habit myself! But go right ahead, liberate yourself from the clutches of thought, and experience a never-before sense of freedom.

> 'We think too much and feel too little.'
>
> —Charlie Chaplin

Small Talk, The Social Lubricant

What to say when you have nothing to tell?

We live in a world smitten by slogans and bowled over by bombast. Where in this obtuse universe of ours will you find a place for those polite noises that go by the self-effacing name of small talk? Alas! It's going to find few takers. But for my money, it's small talk rather than silver-tongued oratory that's going to bail us out of our everyday interactions.

Imagine this: you are standing in line for the elevator along with people with whom you have a nodding acquaintanceship. Saying nothing is one option. Staring fixedly at your mobile and pretending to check WhatsApp messages is another. But neither is going to help you win friends, influence people or at least appear to be a sociable, half-decent guy. Enter small talk. You catch the eye of the person next to you and open the batting. 'Traffic,' you say, 'is getting bad to worse, isn't it?' The other guy nods and possibly shares an update on his own travails about getting to work. By the time quick notes have been exchanged, the lift has reached your floor, and you both go your separate ways. You have converted a stranger into an acquaintance, and small talk has delivered what it was meant to.

For years, I used to dismiss small talk as the handiwork of small minds. At parties and work socials, I kept to myself because I felt I had nothing epoch-making to utter. In the process, I earned an unsavoury reputation. They called me 'stuck-up' and 'snooty' and asked, 'who-does-he-think-he-is?' In desperation, I looked around for remedies, and the solution dawned on me. I needed to make conversation designed not to inform or impress, entertain or enlighten, but simply to fill in the blanks.

Don't let the name fool you. Learning to make small talk is no small accomplishment. You need to tread a fine line between things that are too personal for public airing and fluff, which is so abstract that people will wonder what you are talking about. So beginners can begin with that tried and tested staple—the weather. Yes, this is the mother of all old chestnuts, but it ticks all the boxes as far as your requirements go. It's one-size-fits-all, suitable all year round and for everyone, from boss to buddy to anybody. Most importantly, it's as politically correct as you can get.

But excellent as it is, there will come a time when you tire of observing how hot or cold it has suddenly got, and feel the urge to aim higher. You can then upgrade to commenting upon the days of the week. If it's Monday, you shrug: 'Long, busy week ahead.' If it's Friday, you hit the right notes by enquiring about weekend plans. Keep it light, of course—no need to betray your prurient curiosity.

If you blend small talk with carefully crafted compliments, you get a heady cocktail. All of us love to hear good things about ourselves (we just pretend not to). Latching on to this fundamental truth, the gurus of social interaction tell us to disburse kudos with a liberal hand. Beginning with, 'Hey, nice shirt you are wearing,' you can up the ante to, 'That's a smart little bag you have' or 'What a tan you give your shoes!' You will be surprised how happy you can make people feel by this. One word of caution however: don't overdo the compliments, especially with members of the opposite sex. A 'nice polka dots' is fine, but any ad-libbing about the number and dispersion of those dots can land you squarely in 'Me Too' territory.

Almost as good as a compliment is an engaging question. Online counsellors tell us to ask open-ended questions to draw your listeners out. The questions on offer cover a wide spread—from the popular 'How are you, dear?' to the civil 'What's keeping you busy, young man?' to the slightly corny, 'Sir, who's your favourite author?'

If nothing works, you can always get back to the basics. Simply prepare for small talk like you would for an interview. Before any party, any conference, in fact, before you set out in the morning, prep yourself with things you can small-talk about—news headlines, the cricket score, Bollywood or the raging web serial. A minute's research will also tell you if there's a UN-designated 'World Day' handy.

Such preparation will keep you in touch with whatever is happening, improve your general knowledge and do a world of good for your social standing.

In his autobiography, Stories that I Must Tell, *film star Kabir Bedi attributes his lack of early breakthroughs in Bollywood to his inability to make small talk. He could never bring himself, he says, to chat up film producers and humour them while angling for roles. This went on, till* Sandokan *came along and catapulted Bedi to international stardom and transformed him into the heartthrob of large swathes of women in Europe. Well, you and I are unlikely to have a* Sandokan *moment in our lives. We better hone our small talk skills to help us cruise on the road to our goals.*

Murthy's Law

Avoid guilt. Blame someone.

We all know Murphy's Law. Simply put, it says, 'Anything that can go wrong will go wrong.' Originally formulated at an American aircraft test facility, it has been hailed as a profound truth that fits the human condition like a glove. But that was in the late 1940's, and an update is in order. So make way for Murthy's Law. It states: 'Anything that can go wrong will go wrong…and you are going to be blamed for it.' Who is Murthy, you ask? He is simply the person who, in general opinion is, and always has been, best equipped for taking the blame. Since the law is gender-neutral, it could well be Ms Murthy—but experience has taught me that it is the male of the species who generally cops it.

As children, we gave no time for Murthy's Law to come into effect, for the sound of shattering glass would be directly accompanied by 'Momma, Tannu has broken the tube light.' Or the present continuous tense would be deployed to telling effect: 'Chakori is eating the chocolates.' It was only as time passed and we encountered problems graver than broken tube lights and empty chocolate jars that we realized that there are forces at work that will place you squarely in the crosshairs of fate.

Almost anything can get the law going. At the office, it can range from a typo in the banner welcoming a 'Hor'ble Minister' to your company's gala event ('Couldn't you have got somebody more reliable to proofread?'); or an HR mix-up that resulted in a long-suspended employee getting a surprise promotion. On the domestic front too, the needle of suspicion inevitably swings in a narrowing arc before coming to rest before the third button of your shirt. If the net connectivity is poor, you take the rap ('You are supposed to have gotten this fixed'). Sometimes there is no vulgar finger-pointing, and the people involved are too well-bred for name-calling, but everyone knows whodunnit. When you have taken it upon yourself to organize the food and drinks at your darling niece's wedding reception, and it ends in a spectacular fiasco, even your nearest and dearest ones will pointedly speculate: 'Wonder who selected the caterer?'

US President Dwight Eisenhower had said, 'The search for a scapegoat is the easiest of all hunting expeditions.' There are many abroad who are always ready and willing to join the chase. Since that is how the cookie crumbles, it makes sense to be prepared while the cookies are still in the jar. There are tested ways to soften the impact of Murthy's Law. We all know of the US President (not Eisenhower this time) Harry Truman, who took the blame head-on, with a big 13-inch sign on his desk that read: 'The buck stops here.' Such conspicuous gallantry is okay when you occupy an exalted position. Impeaching the president of the USA is a long-drawn procedure for which nobody these days has the requisite patience or perseverance. But you and I are sackable at short notice. So we need sounder strategies to save our skins and souls.

The first thing you can do is take a bath in Teflon and practise sidestepping blame. For instance, you can commence your defence with a deflective statement along the lines of: 'That family meeting (which ended with raised voices that could be heard nine floors down and woke up the society watchman) was not organized by me but by mama.' Substitute mami, dada, dadi, chacha, chachi…the more distant the relationship, the better. Some people try a different tack. They insure themselves against censure with a Plan B. Their

Plan B is quickly finding whom to blame when Plan A flops. Another method, widely practised at workplaces around the land, is based on simple logic. The more work you do, the more chances you offer the world to pounce upon your errors. So take the elementary precaution of doing as little work as humanly possible.

While such individual efforts can provide some relief, what the world needs today is to revamp the system of looking around for a scapegoat when things go wrong which (as Murphy's Law tells us) is practically all the time. If everyone cooperates, we could institutionalize the entire process. In addition to CEOs, CFOs and COOs, the need of the hour is for a CBO—a Chief Blame Officer. Because he is the one who will get paid to be dragged over the coals, the rest of us can begin to lead our normal lives.

Well, if absolutely none of the above solutions work, don't cry over spilt milk. As they say, it only makes it salty for the cat. Being blamed is not a sign that times are bad or that your Vaastu is defective or that people are ganging up against you, and indeed it is not God's way of punishing you for past misdeeds.

It is simply Murthy's Law.

Shaun Tait, Pakistan's bowling coach, felt the sting of Murthy's Law at a one-day match against England at Lahore in 2022. He was deputed to address the press at the post-match press conference after his team had imploded spectacularly. Tait confessed: 'When we get beaten badly, they send me.'

'Please Adjust'

*In a world of round holes and square pegs,
only adjusting will keep the show going.*

'The quality of mercy,' said Shakespeare's Portia, 'is not strain'd. It droppeth as the gentle rain from heaven upon the place beneath.' Stirring stuff no doubt—the kind of lyricism that gets poets smacking their lips in thrall. But then, poets aren't practical people. In our everyday world, the growing public demand is for less rhetoric and more results. So if Portia were in Vellore or Varanasi, rather than in Venice, you can bet she would have thrown poetry out of the window and, turning to the usurious merchant, intoned a cryptic but compelling: 'Please adjust.'

Although it is not a domestic invention, we Indians have taken to 'adjusting' as if it was designed with our genetic needs in mind. Indeed, if 'adjusting' was an Olympic sport, we would have swept the 'gold', 'silver' and 'bronze' medals. Generally phrased as '*zara* add-just *karo*,' in the northern parts of our country, or '*solpa* adjust *madi*,' in Bangalore and the south, it reflects our accommodative spirit in a universe that is less-than-perfect, and our readiness to move on. 'Adjusting' comes in where corporate strategist Coimbatore Krishnarao Prahalad's 'jugaad' has left off. As you know, 'jugaad' is the Indian way of finding innovative and quick-fix solutions to problems that stump the rest of the world. But what happens when even 'jugaad' doesn't deliver results? Well, you simply adjust.

Adjusting is visible, or more precisely, palpable in the state transport (ST) buses that ply across our fair land. Each bus that plies across the country carries what the Mumbai Suburban Railway officials have defined as 'super dense crush load' (a definition that also applies to all ST buses). En route, the crush load becomes more crushing…until the bus can take no more. But then, the conductor spots a family at the next stop, desperate to get in. Should the bus speed away, leaving the family looking wistfully at the taillights? That would be heartless—and there's also a baby bawling her little heart out. Through practical experience, the conductor knows well the resilience of the human spirit, and equally, the elasticity of the human body. He manages to carve out a mother-and-father-sized hole in the crowd and nods a welcome to the family. As for the bawling baby, he deposits her on the surprised, if not unwelcoming, lap of another mother. That's 'adjusting' in action!

Adjusting applies to all aspects of our lives—from obtaining those certificates that mark both endpoints—birth and death, to everything in between. There are rules and regulations supposedly governing all these activities, but the prevailing view is that only fools will follow rules. Your friendly neighbourhood Chartered Accountant will show you how to get around tax laws, and your railway tout will give you a live demo about how a few minutes of 'adjusting' with the ticket checker can conjure a berth out of thin air. You can also demonstrate your filial regard by 'adjusting' with the health authorities to get your parents an out-of-turn vaccination.

The 'Happy Hour' for adjusting is immediately before and after elections. A close look at the pre-poll preparations will show you many aspirants 'adjusting' with party bosses to bag a ticket. Once the results are out, party ideologies are 'adjusted' beyond recognition as sworn enemies bond overnight to emerge as almost prenatal partners. At the end of it, everyone is happy, leaving the netas laughing all the way to the bank, or, ahem, to their respective hawala operators.

That's why 'adjusting' is called the ultimate 'win-win'.

You and I can never hope to match the mind-numbing records for 'adjusting' set by our politicians. That's not really our fault; it's just that they have a lot more practise. In a country besotted with dynastic politics, netas have an evolutionary head start. Remember Jean-Baptiste Lamarck's giraffe theory? The French scientist told the world that giraffes once had short necks that grew progressively longer as members of each subsequent generation stretched their necks as much as they could to munch the leaves of tall trees. Similarly, our netas have 'adjusted' so often and for so long that their spines have become extraordinarily supple, and in some cases, have disappeared without a trace.

But let's keep transient politicians aside and talk about somebody who's going to be around for some time: you. Ask your friendly neighbourhood freelance psychologists, and they will tell you that at a deep, personal level, 'adjusting' is the key to lasting happiness. Life with all its ups and downs can deflate dreams and sow self-doubt in even the most robust of positive thinkers. Many may then turn bitter with disappointment, but we adjusters, however, are made of sterner stuff. When accomplishments fall short of our aspirations, we simply recalibrate our expectations to suit reality and learn to be content. We seasoned 'adjusters' are also more ready, willing and able to forgive ourselves.

You may not be quite gung-ho about many things around you. People are overbearing, self-centred or lack warmth. Prices of everything could have been lower, and your salary a whole lot higher, your spouse could have been more reasonable, traffic could have been more orderly and you may not be entirely convinced that *achhe din* are here.

Well, please adjust.

> 'We must be willing to let go of the life we planned so as to have the life that is waiting for us.'
>
> —Joseph Campbell

'A' is for the Average

If you are happy enough getting a 'C',
why kill yourself aiming for an 'A'?

Some of the nicest people I know are average, and after deep thought, I have concluded that so am I. For years, I had tried suppressing the evidence, but given my limited abilities, these attempts at appearing brighter than I was misfired most of the time. And then, one day, I had my light bulb moment. I realized that being average was probably the best thing that happened to me.

We of the average fraternity, the original 'A-listers', are comfortable in our skins and better adjusted to society for we are not on an incessant, breathless pursuit of being better than everyone else in sight. And at the end of the day, when we count our blessings, we are generally pleased with the tally. That's more than what can be said for those in the opposite camp, who are divinely dissatisfied, and feel compelled to push themselves, and those around them, on the lines of the seductive but somewhat hazardous Olympic motto—faster, higher, stronger.

I don't know where this fetish for being foremost started. It was perhaps in school where toppers were handled with kid gloves—no scolding, no impositions, and in an age where corporal punishment was part of the curriculum, no public flogging. Parents, too, got into the act by impressing upon me the importance of outshining Neena, Sunil, Keith… At work, come appraisal time, HR departments pulled out the 'bell curve'—an acceptably obscene geometrical figure, which told me in a roundabout way that I needn't expect a bonus that year.

All this has made a lot of people believe that 'average' equals 'bad'. Actually, the average is not a static value. It see-saws, like Sensex on a budget announcement. Think about it—in a team full of stars, your average will also be a star. Conversely, if everyone in class gets 3 out of 10, then that is the average. And talking of all-star teams, they often cut a sorry figure against teams ranked far below them. We cricket lovers should know.

The idea that we, average folk, are not strikingly successful because we lack brains or are not trying hard enough is silly. In this lottery called life, accomplishment has little to do with ability or effort. As the brilliant American physicist Leonard Mlodinow said while commenting on how randomness rules our lives, 'The cord that tethers ability to success is both loose and elastic.' You win some, you lose some—and there's always the law of averages waiting to catch up. What makes things more uncertain is that the mechanism for determining success is notoriously unreliable. Alas, in life, there is no Decision Review System. Even better, there is no Virat Kohli to call out the system and abuse it on the nearest microphone.

It's an unfortunate linguistic aberration that 'mean' denotes both the average as well as a selfish person. Your Mr or Ms Average are anything but mean—they simply don't have the incentive to push everyone aside and reach for the prize. The nasty, 'me first' approach to life is the trademark of super achievers who feel they must come up tops at all costs. The history books won't tell you this but some of the gods we worshipped had not just feet of clay but hearts of stone. They cover a broad spectrum, from Steve Jobs to Henry Ford to dear old Don Bradman. It turns out that they were self-centred and manipulative and if they couldn't push themselves up, were not averse to pulling others down.

Jobs' meanness was incredible. The computer visionary would choose to lie, misrepresent facts, publicly insult, intimidate and be cruel to the people closest to him. All of this is generally forgiven because…well, after all, he was a genius. Automobile legend Henry Ford lost no opportunity to humiliate his son and appointed successor, Edsel, in front of other Ford employees. It is said that company insiders lost count of the number of times the senior Ford had told his son to 'shut up'. As for Bradman, the cricketer, Keith Miller and his other teammates tell us that The Don thought of himself and nobody else. He had a sound cricketing brain but believed that no one else had any brains at all. Again, history forgave and forgot because he had a batting average of ninety-nine. In my book, character is being sacrificed for capability, and that's a terrible price to pay. Just imagine if everyone behaved like them!

The world is a better place with people of moderate ability rather than populated exclusively by 'A' graders. For instance, we should consider ourselves fortunate that those holding the reins of political power happen to be like us, i.e., of middling calibre. How lucky we all are! When average people decide to be wicked, they can go only so far. Think of the consequences if Nero, Hitler and Pol Pot were all geniuses. When the excellent decides to be evil…well, the imagination boggles.

We middle-of-the-roaders rarely grudge those who careen on the fast track, risking life, limb and collateral damage to the soul. After all, who's to argue with personal preferences?

But you can be sure that we at least reach our destinations in good time and are happier along the way. So what's stopping you? As someone said, you will be surprised to find that you are rather good at being average.

> 'I claim to be no more than the average person with less than average capabilities.'
>
> —Mahatma Gandhi

Making the Party Work for You

Get social mileage from every party.

The pandemic and its aftermath have made us forget what a party looks and feels like. We probably wouldn't know what to do if we were invited to one. So while our leaders and betters are busy re-cranking the economy, it's time for us to re-learn a vital survival skill, namely, partying.

First, let's get one thing clear—the objective. If you think the purpose of an office party is for the attendees to have a rollicking time, you are being naive. A party is a marker of social status and provides a platform to prove how popular and charming you are—and how indispensable.

Let's suppose you get an invitation from the Japanese embassy. In terms of snob value, consular parties rank high—only the ones thrown by Bollywood insiders or those hosted on the terraces of Antilia fare better. The occasion could be to greet a master of haiku, but it could be hu tu tu for all you care. You have more important things to attend to, viz., making sure everyone knows where you are going. You can forget to pick up the printout and leave the invitation face up on the printer or your desk. If that doesn't do the trick, you can introduce it gently into conversation. 'This Friday evening I've got to go for that haiku launch,' you say. Or, with a clever touch, you can also say, 'Ah, these Japanese parties go on forever,' making a coveted event sound like some kind of mundane chore you are obliged to carry out. While the occasion, location and dress code may vary, your objective is constant: You are there to make your mark and be recognized as a dapper, socially mobile party animal, adept at making light conversation with guests of both genders. Or rather, looking at the way things are going, make that—guests of *all* genders.

Once in, you can begin to 'work' the crowd. Since parties tend to congeal into little islands, you need to walk deep into the hall and pick the cluster that includes the chief guest and other bigwigs. Also, check the gender balance—all-guy or all-girl groups tend to be dull and made up of losers wishing they were in the other group. The next step is to edge yourself in, play polite listener for a while and when you sense the tiniest of pauses in the flow of conversation, pounce into action.

What do you say? The answer is notable nothings. Unlike the sweet nothings that a boy whispers to a girl and vice versa at the matinee, the nothings at a party are designed to impress rather than express. It doesn't matter if what you say has no connection with what was said previously, and is neither profound nor witty—it won't be understood anyway, especially given the high ambient noise and the low IQs. There is bound to be somebody or the other who will dispute what you say. This should not offend you. It's all part of the intellectual give-and-take that impresses bystanders.

At some parties, you may need to do some role-play. For example, you can play the elder statesman who makes mature observations about Covid, the cosmos and the caffè latte. Or you could be the resident wit whose responsibility is to make everyone laugh incessantly. You could even throw caution and common manners to the wind and awaken your inner Arnab. Interrogate those around you, but squelch them before they can speak. You will draw in a large audience—if only for the entertainment value. Groups are also in dire need of somebody they can laugh at, and you could be the sporting volunteer. As the butt of all jokes, there will be a lot of fun at your expense, but you can bet that you will always be in the limelight.

Now, to the refreshments. The good news is that parties are generally flush with exotic food and single malts. The bad news is that you must not take as much of either as you would have loved to. This may be hard to stomach—both literally and figuratively—but it is vital if you want to make your mark. The fact is, our weird old world looks up in awe at gourmands and looks down contemptuously on gluttons. So hold yourself back from making a grab at everything from fish fingers to falooda.

Remember how you made a strategic entry into the party? Well, even more important than your entry is how you time your exit. You score big when you excuse yourself midway, saying you have an appointment that you can't miss, or better still, another party to attend. Nothing impresses the general public as much as the hotshot who can give the ras malai a miss.

The acquaintances you form at one party will turn into your bosom friends at the next, and before long you will soon build a network of partygoers that is the envy of lesser mortals. Hurrah! You've arrived!

> 'The bad news is time flies.
> The good news is you're the pilot.'

—Michael Altshuler

9 to 5

That blessing in disguise.

This is a universal gripe. People complain that they never seem to have enough time for themselves. Not enough time to read, paint, do Sudoku, talk to their friends or flowers, collect stamps or shells, play the violin, or just let their hair down and get together with friends. The villain behind all this is the usual suspect, the 9-to-5 routine, which robs us of most of our waking hours. If only we knew what really happens, we wouldn't be ruing our plight. Instead, we would be bringing out the bubbly.

Yes, you heard that right. Having limited time is actually a stroke of good luck—because if we were given all the time in the world to do the things we love, maybe we wouldn't love them so much anymore. Look at it this way—you like spending an occasional morning playing 'tennis ball cricket' with the kids in the lane. But imagine if that's all there is to do through the day—gully cricket from dawn to dusk. Even the most besotted lover of the game would call for a strategic time-out. Just as we are careful to not overstay the hospitality of our hosts, we ought to take care we don't overstay the hospitality of our hobbies.

Many of us learnt the hidden value of limited time during the lockdown imposed by fate and the local administration during the pandemic. Those whining about the lack of time suddenly found mountains of it, much more than they knew what to do with. A couple of years ago, a colleague who worked long hours at the office would often tell me that he wished he had more time for his little children. How he would have loved to have them around, join them in their games, answer their million questions, tell them stories and generally watch them grow. During the pandemic, his wish was answered, through the divine agency of 'work from home'. The first week passed in a whirl of video games and high-spirited whoops. By the end of the second week, the novelty of having Papa around all the time was wearing thin, but they soldiered on. By month end, it was obvious to all concerned that it was much better having Bittu, Sid and Monu as playtime companions. As for Papa himself, he was veering towards the opinion that those assignments at the office weren't so bad after all.

The regular office regimen may seem heartless but it helps the indecisive individuals (and their number is legion). It helps them make up their minds. It tells them how much time they must allot for work. The rest is 'my time', to fill in as you please. What happens when you do not have the advantage of a set 9-to-5 routine for yourself? Well, a vacation without start and end dates won't seem like a vacation for too long.

The problem begins when we imagine ourselves to be the creative sort who cannot stick to deadlines and for whom 'time' is a four-letter word. We could persuade ourselves that our talent should never be force-fit into little slots in a timetable. That, unfortunately, is a con game we play upon ourselves. The back stories of some of the most successful members of the 'creative' tribe reveal that they subscribe to a cast iron schedule themselves. Haruki Murakami has set himself a rigid schedule and says: 'I keep to this routine every day without variation. The repetition itself becomes the important thing; it's a form of mesmerism. I mesmerize myself to reach a deeper state of mind.'

What's true for hobbies and pastimes also holds good at a different level for happiness. The delight we derive from our off-beat interests is inversely proportionate to the time we can spare for them. Having all the time in the world to sketch, sew, read or ride can dilute our passions. To enjoy a break from a routine, you need to have a routine in the first place.

Despite all this, it may still be difficult to convince ourselves that we are better off the way we are. Our heart is always reluctant to listen to our head. So we will probably hate it when we are compelled to put the book or bicycle away because of the urgent summons of duty. Yes, you can still grouch and wish you could find plenty of time to indulge in your hobbies. Just pray that your wishes never come true.

> 'The secret of your future is hidden
> in your daily routine.'
>
> —Mike Murdock

The Fine Art of Flattery

If some men are born great, others ingratiate.

MAN DOESN'T LIVE BY BREAD ALONE. HE NEEDS BUTTERING.

Blowing your own trumpet is bad manners, but you can outsource that role to others and become the cause of much joy all around. The flatterers will be happy in the knowledge that their gushing torrent is being accepted at face value—and that their axes will soon be ground. As for the recipients of the aural massage, while they may pretend to be dismissive of all this fuss, they are thrilled to bits too and are actually hoping for more. In these stressful times, what better formula can you find for disseminating good cheer?

Despite such excellent references, flattery, unfortunately, has fallen foul of the conscience keepers. It has been branded insincere as it gives the audience a false positive result. Its manipulative purveyors are said to switch sides depending on which way the wind blows. 'He who knows how to flatter,' warned Napoleon, 'will also know how to slander.' It took a scholar and counter-intuitive thinker, Professor Daniel J. Kapust, to present a more mature, balanced view. In *Flattery and the History of Political Thought*, Kapust points to a distinction between two kinds of flatterers, viz., the 'cunning flatterers and dependent flatterers'. The puffery of the 'dependent flatterer' is not driven by avarice but the 'precariousness of their social status'. When your life, future and all things precious are poised on the brink, you don't mind gilding the truth a good bit.

When it's not a life-or-death struggle, apple polishing can be a labour-saving device—probably history's oldest. Man has always had an inflatable ego. I am sure back in the day, when Madam Cavewoman needed the logs to be brought in, or the sabre-toothed tiger at the door to be sorted out, she would have cosied up to Mr Caveman and called him a hunk— the hunkiest in the Savannah. Modernity has delivered other options to eliminate labour: dishwashers, washing machines, mixer grinders... (Matter of fact, even the shower saves you from having to do calisthenic exercises with bathroom mugs). But machines cost money and need to be periodically maintained (my shower has been dripping for months). Flattery comes with no such encumbrances.

So this leaves you with two ways to please the powers that be. At home, you can opt to dust the house, clear the loft, drive to the market and bring in the groceries. At the workplace, you can work late hours, stand in for colleagues who have reported sick and volunteer for duties nobody else wants to do. Or you can put it all aside and simply tell your wife/boss/ mother-in-law what an absolutely wonderful person they are.

Which option do you think is more attractive and easier?

As a long-standing flatterer, let me warn you that the flatteratzzi these days are running into all kinds of problems. The biggest among them is competition. There are just too many of our tribe around for our own song of praise to reach the intended ears. Also, fulsome, full-frontal flattery is losing its efficacy due to over-harvesting, and there have been cases reported of people who have developed immunity.

Welcome then, to Flattery 3.0.

In this new variant, you do things differently. You steer clear of mainstream adjectives, namely, best, greatest, wisest, noblest and most wonderful. You bypass such superlatives because, ugh, you don't want to advertise your intentions and go over the top. Instead, you construct your sentence differently and couple it with non-verbal indications of admiration. You say: 'We have been trying to tackle this wretched problem for years, and here you (the target) come, and suddenly...poof!' Conclude with an appropriate gesture. Alternatively, you can puff up the person's background rather than his personal accomplishments. 'I think it's your long years in the army that have helped you stand up to that crowd.' Putting in a good word about the subject's parents goes down well too. Consider, for example, 'I'm sure you learnt to make this fish curry from your mother!' On the other side of the family, you can deduce that your subject's distinct and gravelly voice clearly comes from his father's ability to warble Saigal.

An even more imaginative method is to say nothing about the target and speak about his protégés aka chelas. 'Your boys are very good. You can tell who their mentor is.' This follows the old Bollywood line of thought: *Bade miyan toh bade miyan, chhote miyan subhan Allah.* (The master is, well, the master, but as for the junior ... God be praised!) A word of caution, however. Be discerning in your choice of when and whom to extol. Promiscuous flatterers who carpet-bomb everyone with praise will find their words demonetized.

So there you have it. Flattery is a career accelerator, peacemaker, incentivizer for better results, resolver of deadlocks, promoter of good relations and the most efficient contributor to gross national happiness. We owe this 'glib and oily art' a round of applause. In other words, it is time we began showering flattery with richly deserved praise.

So here goes. Hail to thee, God's gift to human discourse. You are music to the ears and balm for hurt souls. May your honeyed words get sweeter with age and your ornate ways gild our spirits. For man doth not live by bread alone, he needs buttering up.

A newly-crowned Nizam remarked at lunch that the eggplant was a tasty vegetable. All his courtiers nodded and said that the 'brinjal was the most delicious vegetable in the kingdom and the finest example of divine bounty.' But, continued the Nizam, its shape is crude, and would not please the eye of an artist. At this, the courtiers called the vegetable a blight that ought to be banished from human sight. The Nizam appeared puzzled. He said, 'You are funny people. When I say something is good, you praise it to the skies. When I say that the same thing just looks bad, you condemn it. Why is that?' There was an uneasy silence all around. Nobody said a word until the oldest courtier mustered courage. 'The reason is simple, your Highness,' he said, 'we eat your salt, not the salt of the brinjal.'

Life's a Bargain

Let's have more action in your every transaction.

I rarely experience as much undiluted joy as at the euphoric moment when I strike a terrific bargain. Only seasoned bargainers among you will understand this. Non-bargainers will ask irritating questions, like how much money did you ultimately save after all that wrangling, but that is beside the point. Those who have cut their teeth on Mumbai's Linking Road or in the legendary Chor Bazaar or their honourable counterparts in other cities will vouch that winning an intense game of negotiating feels like a million dollars, even if you only win a few rupees. You bargain for the thrill of it, and it is no more a means to an end than taking a walk along Marine Drive is a means to understanding oceanography.

It is said that you can tell a person's character by the way he opens a sealed envelope. But you can understand character more thoroughly by watching a live bargain. On Mumbai's Fashion Street, for a T-shirt tagged ₹110, if you tentatively propose ₹100, hoping all the while that you are not causing offence, you are a kind human being of tender disposition.

But you would be better off in a fair-price shop. If, however, you turn the hawker apoplectic by holding out 35 rupees as your last offer, you truly belong to our tribe.

Welcome to the blood sport of bargaining!

A gently-spoken Danish industrialist had once said that no deal must be concluded except between a happy buyer and a happy seller. But such sweet sentiments belong to another age. Today, self-interest reigns paramount, and we subscribe to what Albert Camus said, 'to be happy, we must not be too concerned with others.' If cricket is war minus the shooting, bargaining is a duel minus the swords. Its twists and turns bring out our hidden talents: patience and perseverance, the skill to plot moves like a grandmaster and our histrionic ability to stagger and faint at hearing the going price of an 'authentic' Tanjore painting.

There is a scientific technique to low-risk, high-reward bargaining and there are books and online material to tell you how to put it into practice. The first thing to do is camouflage your intentions. If you enter a gem store in Hyderabad looking for a coral set, you must look at everything except corals. Your decoy could well be a pearl necklace, expensive enough to mark you out as a likely big spender. After carefully studying the pearls against the light, you keep them aside for the moment and ask for specimens of garnets, sapphires, lemon quartz and pearls. Almost as an afterthought, you toss in the corals too. Once you've got a radiant heap on the counter, it's time to haggle for discounts on each type. Now, you will find out what the individual items are really worth (in technical negotiations, this is called 'price discovery'). Brimming with bravado, you go straight for the jugular. Swiftly discarding the other items as not to your taste, and adding that you have a flight to catch soon, you are left with the discounted corals you wanted. You get them packed and walk away before the storekeeper can read the game.

Well, this is how the classic formula goes, but the reader is advised discretion. It's quite probable the shopkeeper may have gone through the same book and the same website.

If you don't feel up to no-holds-barred bargaining right now, you can accompany your more hard-nosed friends on shopping expeditions to pick up useful tips. You will learn human psychology, mind reading and market trends. Most importantly, bargaining will teach you about the ups and downs of fate.

When you look at it critically, life is our long bargain with the forces of the universe. To get anything, you need to give something in return—whether it's at school, workplace, on the sports field or house of worship. Happiness or sorrow is the outcome of how favourable your transaction turned out to be. We learn this lesson early in life and then pass it on to our children. We may use our discretion and not spell things out, but the message is clear to all—be a good boy or girl and the world will respect you; study long and hard and become prosperous doctors or software engineers and go to the USA.

As in a flea market, so in life, there are no permanent winners, no permanent losers. At the sabzi mandi, what you win on the cauliflowers, you could lose on beans and bitter gourd. It's possible that the antique water pot, which you were assured is hand-carved, could turn out to be machine-made at the neighbouring industrial gala. That is how the cookie crumbles. Even ace bargainers have been scalped on their off days. (It happens with every sport. Think back to the long periods when Virat Kohli and Sachin got out to poor scores.)

When realization dawns that we have been sold a dummy, we bargainers don't get into a sulk or swear to confine ourselves to the fair-price shop.

We live to bargain another day.

> 'We must accept finite disappointment,
> but never lose infinite hope.'
>
> —Martin Luther King Jr.

God Help Us with Our Faith!

Will someone please turn the thermostat back to normal?

Religion has been a touchy topic, even during the best of times. But these days, room temperatures are set at a simmer, and even making casual conversation about matters of faith can have explosive consequences. Discussing religion is, as P.G. Wodehouse would have put it, like looking for the leak in a gas pipe using a lighted candle. People who you thought were moderate and level-headed—people you counted as friends have not just turned tetchy; they seem to revel in their new-found fervour. What's come over us? For all practical purposes, some of us seem to have mutated into fundamentalists under our skins.

This closet variant is even more toxic than the ones who wear their bigotry on their sleeves. You won't catch the asymptomatic fundamentalist throwing stones at places of worship other than their own, but their prejudices are at work unobtrusively and insidiously. Many of them nurture the unexpressed belief that their chosen God is markedly superior ('new and improved!') to others. Ergo, they themselves are a cut above the rest. While they will tolerate no light-hearted comments about their own practices, they are not above snide remarks or condescending glances at the oddball rituals of others. And let's face it, every faith has a handful of those.

Speaking solely for myself, I believe that in this world of ours, there is enough space for all opinions, ideologies and systems of belief. I have been sceptical of the arrogant assumptions about faith and the somewhat insolent idea that a single system of belief alone has all the answers. Also, the more ostentatious practices of religion remind me of Konstantin Stanislavski's school of method acting, where you keep practising certain gestures, hoping to generate the required emotion. (I always wonder why God can't see through the pantomime.) Such excesses of piety are usually the first step on the slippery slope to bigotry, and soon you will be so busy with God that you will have no time for your fellowmen. But then all this is just my own view—am probably biased and perhaps ill-informed, and I cannot let my truth deny yours.

Trouble starts when you are overzealous about your religion, and the other fellow decides that he had better be overzealous too, lest his God feels left out (we are adept at transferring human insecurities to our deities). Before we know it, we have a divinity derby going. Competition will do to faith what it has done to the economy—shift attention to the packaging rather than to the product. So we will want our religious procession to be longer than the others, our pennants taller, cymbals louder, our prayers longer… And yes, with all this, down goes our tolerance threshold for books, paintings, cartoons, films and serials that may depart from the straight and the narrow.

A friend of mine once told me that although he was a conservative Brahmin by birth, he used to be okay with eating the odd tandoori chicken. But one day, he found a colleague scrupulously avoiding meat that was not halal. My friend then started thinking—if his colleague could be so steadfast, surely he owed it to his own faith to demonstrate his allegiance as well. He promptly struck tandoori chicken off his menu for life.

It's not just chicken that he is missing out on now. There is a lot in the rainbow of life that is denied to us when we adopt a rigorous (dare I say, 'blinkered') approach. It is ultimately a broad, all-embracing stance, which opens windows all around us. In the pressure-cooker atmosphere we live in, even well-meaning people can let prejudices seep into their systems. Here is a spot check to find out your secular quotient.

Ask yourself who your favourites are from different fields: best actor, singer, poet, scientist, doctor, cricketer, Olympic athlete or public personality of any stripe. If you find that for one reason or another, the majority of them belong to your own community or region, I am afraid your liberal quotient is low, and the tank is running on 'empty'. The solution is simple, and entirely up to you. Step out of the mental boundary lines that you may have unconsciously drawn for yourself and deliberately cultivate heroes and role models from farther afield. You will discover riches you did not know existed.

Before the next OTT serial, stand-up comedian or book kicks up controversy afresh, perhaps it is time we stepped back and replayed in our minds the beautiful words of Dr John Sentamu, the first black African archbishop of the Church of England. Addressing his flock, he had said, 'We have lost the joy and power that makes real disciples and we've become consumers of religion…' He urged them therefore to, '…go and find friends among Buddhists, Hindus, Jews, Muslims, Sikhs, agnostics, atheists, not for the purpose of converting them to your beliefs but for friendship, understanding, listening, hearing.'

Centuries ago, Leigh Hunt had put much the same sentiment into poetry. His Abou Ben Adhem did not make it to the angel's shortlist of the people who loved God the most. That list would have contained the usual suspects: fundamentalists of all stripes, the intolerant and the assertive champions of the 'my way or the highway' strain of religion… But he consoled himself by loving his fellowmen, and as we all know, that when the angel reappeared with a more relevant roll call, a list of those whom God had blessed, sure enough, Adhem's name was right on top.

That's the way to go, I feel. And if none of this works, heaven help us.

> 'The belief that one's own view of reality is the only reality is the most dangerous of all delusions.'
>
> —Paul Watzlawick

A Toast to the Boast!

When the truth becomes tedious,
it's time for bluffers to do their bit.

We've heard a lot of pre-poll promises, and we know from experience that they have a lifespan shorter than morning dew. But that doesn't deter our netas from freely dispensing claims, and dishing out promises and assurances. Jobs are going to materialize out of nowhere, 'outsiders' are going to be kicked out with nothing but the clothes on their backs, corrupt officials are going to be kicked out with nothing but their crores in tax havens, roads are going to be paved before you can say 'pothole', an airport will come up there, a factory here and a children's recreation park in between. And before I forget, our economy is going to become so big, you will lose count of the zeroes.

I don't know about you but all of this is music to my ears. The taller the claim, the more I admire the claimant; the bigger and more extravagant the promise, the more I applaud the neta making it. This drab, dreary world of ours needs perking up, and the only ones who can do it are bluffers, braggarts, 'fekus' and what-have-yous.

Politics is generally seen as having the biggest braggarts but other fields are not far behind. At home, there is always the cousin who regales the family with his feats in faraway lands. Or there's the aunt who brags about her old prawn pickle that had grown men literally eating out of her hands. At work, there are ambitious executives whose descriptions of their own accomplishments during self-appraisals read like pages from Homer. And then, there are management consultants! They remind me of Mark Twain talking about a hen, which after laying just an egg, cackles as if it has laid an asteroid. But wherever they are and whatever they say, every bluffer is doing society a service by adding to the gaiety of public discourse.

Imagine if your WhatsApp group was populated entirely by Raja Harishchandras (aiyyo!) and the odd George Washington (yawn…). Can you imagine scrolling down reams and reams of factual but intimidatingly dull posts on the plight of the world? It won't be long before you leave the group and look for an alternative whose members are—how do I put it—a bit more adventurous with the truth? Those who only speak the truth have made a name for themselves, like the illustrious gentlemen quoted earlier in this paragraph. But equally, the roll call of liars is long and illustrious.

A book on Italian filmmaker, and arguably the 'GOAT' in world cinema, Federico Fellini, was titled: *I'm a Born Liar*. How appropriate! In the field of politics, heading the pack of accomplished liars is Henry Kissinger, who at one time was the power behind the throne in Nixon's USA. Of Kissinger, it was said that 'he lies not because it is in his interest but because it is in his nature.'

Tall talkers see the world not as it is, but as it might have been had inconvenient circumstances not interfered. I, for instance, might well have been putting up at the toniest part of Mumbai had Andheri not usurped its place. I might have been owning a Mercedes-S Coupé, had an endless succession of 'share-taxis' and autorickshaws not gotten here first. By now, I might have been a best-selling humourist had the public's adamant refusal to find my writings funny not nipped my plans in the bud. I might have…the list goes on. Are such illusions the approaching signs of going loony? Well, I will go with the immortal words of the man of La Mancha, Don Quixote: 'Perhaps to be too practical is madness. To surrender dreams—this may be madness. Too much sanity may be madness—and maddest of all:

to see life as it is, and not as it should be!'

The way life pans out, reality almost always falls short of the ideal. Seeing this, lesser mortals will wring their hands in despair, sulk or blame their spouses and the prime minister. But we bluffers make up the shortfall with a generous scoop of imagination. Trouble starts to brew because there are people around who do not possess our level of imagination. These spoilsports point a finger at flaws and deficiencies and complain, for instance, that the 'din' are not as 'acche' as we were assured they would be. Use your imagination, guys! Remember what Albert Einstein had said: 'Imagination is more important than knowledge.' And if you want corroboration from a more recent and far superior physicist, log in to the orange-robed Swami Nithyananda, who dresses drivel in scientific clothes with such aplomb that you won't know which is which.

Truth is noble and nice but it can be trite. Similarly, humility is a wonderful virtue, but you shouldn't go overboard with it. Or blame someone for not playing by your rules. Does it really matter if someone likes the sonorous blast of his own trumpet?

I would go in the opposite direction. If a man persists with his humility and refuses to blow his own trumpet, I will doubt not just his lung power but the value of his accomplishments. As Winston Churchill said of the hapless Clement Attlee, 'he is a modest man—with much to be modest about.'

And finally, I wish the world would be more appreciative of the efforts we bluffers put into our roles. Telling the truth is a relatively simpler job; it takes guts, of course, but that's about it. In contrast, camouflaging the truth, and keeping the game going for any length of time calls for craft and the calculating mind of a chess grandmaster. India's mercurial diplomat and ill-starred Defence Minister Krishna Menon is supposed to have said that it takes intelligence to be able to tell a good lie. Well, this information comes from the illustrious editor of the *Illustrated Weekly*, the late Khushwant Singh. So I leave it to you to answer the question—who was bluffing whom?

> 'Never believe anything about the government until it is officially denied.'
>
> —Anonymous

Unplugging Nostalgia

Those good old days—were they really that good?

Is your favourite singer K.L. Saigal? Do you believe no one played the square cut better than G.R. Viswanath? And was the best payasam ever made the one that granny used to conjure up on your birthdays? If you have ticked 'Yes' to any of these questions, your mental calendar has more yesterdays than is good for you. Worse, dear reader, you could also be suffering from a mild form of mental illness.

'Nostalgitis' is contagious—as transmissible as the virus you don't need to be reminded about. When your family or friends get talking about the golden days gone by, so will you. A class reunion or an assembly of middle-aged relatives is a nostalgia hotspot. We go: 'Remember the way chacha used to snort?' or 'I still crack up when I think of our French teacher trying to get us to do the verbs.' All this is great fun, of course, but it's the kind of fun that has a built-in time limit. How long can you keep entertaining each other with memories of the past?

The hard question to ask is—was any of it true? Were those good old days really all that good?

In the back of our minds, we are all in a way conscious that we are being judicious with the truth, intuitively selecting what to save and what to delete. We airbrush the unpleasantness, gloss over those petty jealousies that ran inches beneath the surface and blank out the pinpricks and the pain. As Proust said, 'Remembrance of things past is not necessarily the remembrance of things as they were.'

Nostalgia works only when a minimum duration of time has elapsed. Nobody gets nostalgic about yesterday or last Sunday. It is customary to leave a healthy fifteen- to twenty-year gap—a mental form of social distancing—from the events that we talk about. That is time enough for our minds to soften the rough edges and sugar-coat remembrances. There is also a protocol to be followed: we are not supposed to examine anybody's memories under the microscope. When someone paints a rose-tinted portrait of their 'carefree college days', it is bad form to remind them of the anxieties of their early days on the campus. When someone drools about those wonderful days at the start of their career, it's not done to pour cold water on their recollections by pointing out that office politics was as rife then as it is now. Why then are we taken up with the good old days when we know that much of it is as fake as a Donald Trump pronouncement? Because sometimes, we love to lie to ourselves, and when the present is uncomfortable, it's tempting to seek refuge in a reimagined past.

Nostalgia is a form of escapism, much like a Karan Johar film. By itself, that should not deter us. Considering the times we live in, escaping into a fantasy world is sometimes the most sensible option. But the difference is that we know exactly what Karan Johar is up to, and once his gilded tale is over, we switch back on and get back to the real world. Nostalgia addicts, however, never make the effort to step out of their make-believe world because, in the first place, they do not admit that they are occupying a Never Never Land.

If left unchecked, nostalgia can easily become toxic. It can make you turn your nose up at everything happening around you. A fine piece of modern architecture? This is nothing. You should see those buildings built by the Brits in the neo-Gothic style. A witty piece by a humour writer? *Shee, shee*! It's not in the same league as P.G. Wodehouse or Jerome K. Jerome. A modern gadget that saves time and hard labour? This generation wants everything easy—I still do it the old way. It takes time, of course, but you will never get the same results with this newfangled contraption.

Often, nostalgia is a trigger for exaggeration. Things were so much better back in the day, and are so terrible now. Actually, neither extreme will stand up to scrutiny. Nostalgia is also an age marker—make no mistake. Only the aged dwell in the past. Ever seen a ten-year-old spending quality time musing about the days when they were five? In its extreme form, it can deprive you of the motivation to do anything serious about improving your lot. If the best days are long past, why make the effort to try and change anything?

Should we then get rid of all sepia-tinted thoughts the way we do with spam mail? And while we are at it, should we also log out of all those online groups that are getting so popular on the net, e.g., 'Old Xavierites', 'Old Bombay' and 'Old Melodies'? Such drastic action would certainly sanitize our minds, but it could also turn them sterile. Psychologists say that memories can sometimes be a source of inspiration.

So the smart thing to do would be to change gears and step back into the present every time we sortie into the past. The widely-respected journal, *Psychology Today,* recommends that we connect our past with our present without comparing the two. So saying, 'Things are terrible now', and leaving it at that is to imprison yourself in the past. Instead, look at both past and present, and try and connect the dots. You may remember the times when you used to regale your friends with your songs. Well, what's stopping you from dusting off the old guitar, calling friends over and singing a new number?

So strum your way into a future that's sure to be as lilting as the past. There are no expiry dates on happiness, and the best days of your life could well be ahead of you. Bid a polite goodbye then to nostalgia, and start living actively in the present. You will soon find that you are doing the things today that you can be nostalgic about the day after.

Maverick Marathi poet, Vinda Karandikar, told us about an old man who 'in his youth had pissed into the ocean, and then spent the rest of his life trying to measure the rise in water level.' That's what unchecked nostalgia can do to people!

Procrastination versus Anti-crastination

*We never shirk work; we only
wait for the right time to start.*

This world of ours is full of 'anti-crastinators'. They are the ones goading us with their incessant 'do it nows' and cracking the whip on us peaceful procrastinators. There is more bad news on the way. The 'anti-crastinators' have cornered all the key jobs—from managing directors to mukadams around the country, and for good measure, have grabbed positions of power in the domestic circuit as well as mothers/fathers-in-law, uncles and aunts. Before long, your spouse will join forces with them too. This means that life could become one long 'To Do' list and the world will run pretty much on the unrealistic, unnecessary deadlines they set. It also means that people still won't get the vital difference between procrastinators and shirkers.

To clarify, procrastinators stand much higher up the food chain. Unlike shirkers, we don't avoid work, we are only waiting for the right moment to do it. Unfortunately, those who swear by deadlines swear at those who don't. It strikes me as strange that a world that places so much importance on getting the right hour and precise minute to conduct weddings, inaugurations and ceremonial visits goes lax about any muhurat when it comes to work. But we procrastinators can't afford to be so nonchalant. So when you see us lolling around on the sofa instead of completing that project report, it's because the muhurat hasn't yet struck us as being just right.

We, Indians, have been viewing time as a relative concept long before Einstein came up with the idea. The joke about IST—Indian Stretchable Time—is something we all grew up with. But it's not Indians alone—procrastinators can form an elite international group. Former US president Bill Clinton was described by his Vice President as 'punctuality challenged'. Leonardo da Vinci waited for sixteen years before he felt he had got the smile on the lady right. I bet if today's time management experts had been snapping at his heels, Mona Lisa would have ended up bang on schedule but would be indistinguishable from a Bollywood film poster. Mozart was one of us too, and his views on the subject of postponing his creations should be music to our ears.

It was English poet and philosopher, Edward Young, who was the outlier. He stigmatized our noble vocation with 'procrastination is the thief of time'. (Charles Dickens is also credited with this line, but he only made it popular.) So let me give you Young's backstory. He wrote during an age when poets had to be supported by patrons. If they had had television in those days, you could expect to see, 'This part of the poem is sponsored by the Earl of Berkshire.'

Our Young was very good when it came to impressing the opulent class and persuading them to agree to loosen their purse strings and dish out patronage. But for one reason or another, the largesse rarely lasted. In one case, the poet had pinned all his hopes on a wealthy merchant who agreed to provide funds. As luck would have it, the ink on the agreements had hardly dried before the potential benefactor's businesses failed and the promised patronage never came through. If only Young had put off signing the deal and waited to see how his potential patron was faring on the business front, he would have ended up a richer man—and we, proponents of postponing, would have escaped public criticism.

Excessive and undue punctuality, I have always believed, is somewhat inconsiderate to our fellow human beings. You remember those teacher's pets in school who used to turn in their homework bright and early, just to go one up on the rest of the class? Some people have retained this streak of meanness all their lives. They achieve their quarterly targets well in time; they are on track with their social and professional calendars and they may never ever know what it is to miss a deadline. They could be role models for a happy life, but I doubt if it is really as happy as it is made out to be. The way I see it, these guys are procrastinators too—the only thing is that they are procrastinating the enjoyment of life. Now, who do you think has made the wiser choice? As someone said the other day: it is debatable if the early bird enjoys the worm as much as the late bird enjoys the extra sleep!

You will be happy to know that the Gods look down indulgently on our tribe, and forgive us our many errors of omission. Let's say your wife has asked you to clear the loft. You readily recognize its importance—cluttered lofts are a superspreader of ants, cockroaches and other undesirables. Worse, they also displease the goddess of wealth, and who among us is man enough to risk incurring Her wrath! But for one reason or another, you put off the task, lightly overlooking your wife's reminders. The reasons for being 'unpunctual' are also valid: your back has been hurting, you need a longer broom and you have not yet found a place to store those old issues of Readers' Digest. After a month or so, you will find that the loft has been cleared. No point in enquiring about the details. Obviously, there is some cosmic labour-saving device at work—yes, the Force is with us.

Now, there may be those among us who are uncomfortable with all the above. They do not want a 'To Do' list preying on their minds. In other words, they want to gradually (if not indeed *this* minute) stop being procrastinators. Well, we respect their choice and will even go out of our way to point out the many methods of overcoming the urge to put off things. There's the 'Clock Lock' method where you tell yourself that you are going to get cracking on a job at a particular time, say, 11 p.m. Once you have put it down in your mental diary, don't let anything come in the way. Then there is the 'Instalment Plan'. Here, you divide large and intimidating jobs into Estimated Monthly Instalments, or even, Estimated Daily Instalments. You are less likely to procrastinate if it is a small job that you *can* tackle. To keep motivation levels high, psychologists say that you should also reward yourself for completing a task you have taken on. A single malt should be a potent incentive.

There you have it. Which road should you follow—be prompt or procrastinate? That's a vital decision, and it is one that you need to take on your own.

If you still can't make up your mind, turn to that unfailing fount of wisdom—vintage Bollywood. A timeless Raj Kapoor classic has this gem, *'Aaj ka kaam kal karo, kal ka kaam parson; itni jaldi kya hai, jab jeena hai barson?'* (Put off to tomorrow what you are supposed to do today. We are going to be around for years so what's the big hurry anyway!) It's time we changed the world's image about ourselves with a Procrastinators' Manifesto. I promise I will get down to writing it this afternoon. Or perhaps tomorrow...or most definitely this Sunday.

> 'Tomorrow—a mystical land where 99 per cent of all human productivity, motivation and achievement is stored.'
>
> —Anonymous

Do Less, Delegate More

Work is such a noble thing,
you shouldn't keep it all for yourself.

Why do you think large, high-level teams representing companies and countries, associations and affiliations are called delegations? Simple, because its members delegate and do little else. Should we pull up these idlers and demand some accountability?

Relax.

If you ask me, the world would be better off with more of their kind. They may look and behave like champion passers of parcels, but there's more to delegation than meets the eye.

I learnt what it takes early in life from my father, a seasoned delegator who earned his spurs in a public sector undertaking. Among the few things Dad chose to take upon himself, rather than delegate to my mother, was to teach me survival techniques in the big bad world. With deft sleight of hand, he showed how unwelcome work could be magically deflected towards unsuspecting colleagues further down the food chain.

Let's say your department is tasked with digitizing office archives. It's a thankless, soul-killing chore, ridden with problems and pitfalls. In other words, it is a job better done by somebody—anybody—other than you. Now, baldly stating that the tiresome task be passed to meek and mild Mani slaving away in the department's boondocks is giving the game away. Instead, you spread the word in advance that sorting out archives is a specialized job, one which calls for a meticulous mind and a high degree of application. You will add that Mani is endowed with just such a mind. Before he knows it, the job, with an elongated trail of emails and varied attachments, will have lodged itself inextricably in Mani's inbox.

To be an accomplished delegator, you need to look the part. It won't do to be seen lounging around and chatting amiably by the water cooler, with no visible indications of or inclinations towards productive activity. That is why smart delegators manage to look constantly busy and preoccupied with higher responsibilities. Nobody will actually pause to find out what exactly those responsibilities are so long as you maintain the air of the one carrying the world on your shoulders while simultaneously orchestrating the efforts of the minions in your troupe. Take a leaf from the king of the jungle. The lion's brooding air of menace is enough to make sure that the hard slog of hunting prey is pushed towards others in the pack, even while he continues to enjoy the lion's share.

Now suppose you lack such regal looks and the personality that is a prerequisite for getting others to do work. Worry not, there is an even simpler way. Just slip out of the line of sight when you sense that the boss is going to hand out the day's chores. Take the day off, disappear into another department, another office, another city. As a last resort, you could even attempt ducking under your desk. Remember what you learnt in childhood—the parcel can't be passed to someone who can't be seen.

The gold medal in the Delegation Olympics goes to the boss who succeeds in making the job that needs to be plonked on someone's plate seem like a prestige assignment. In my time, I have dangled the most boring jobs tantalizingly in front of starry-eyed juniors eager to embellish their CVs. When executed with finesse, this strategy is a classic win-win, delighting both delegator and delegatee. The relief that the delegator experiences in getting a job off his back is nothing compared to the pride that the delegatee feels as he convinces himself that he is being marked out for special attention (as in a possible promotion).

Delegation also comes to your rescue if things go wrong, as they often will. Since you are not handling the job yourself, delegation gives you the sense of detachment to analyse the causes and apportion blame fairly, squarely and loudly. In contrast, if things pan out perfectly, you can step forth and accept praise as your due. After all, there is a limit on how much you ought to delegate!

As an evangelist of redirecting responsibilities, I believe our world would have been a happier place if folks in high places had delegated more and done less. Here is my wish list: if only Chinese Premier Xi Jinping had delegated the task of managing viruses and vials in Wuhan to more capable hands. And yes, to our west, I wish the Generals of Pakistan to delegate the work of running the country to those elected for the purpose—hapless Prime Ministers. Closer home, I wish our public intellectuals (an endangered species) delegate writing insightful articles about the government to professionals more qualified for the job say, IPL cheerleaders. I also look forward to the day when ministers in states around the country get a clear idea about their responsibilities. They could delegate to lesser mortals the task of advising us on the kind of jeans we ought to wear, what to eat, which books to read and which films to see. With somebody else taking care of such matters, they will suddenly find a lot more time to do what, in the rush of things, could have slipped their mind, i.e., administer.

Of course, I was always a bit uncomfortable with the word itself because, since the early 1970s any word suffixed with 'gate' has become synonymous with skulduggery. But I now realize that it aptly describes the work ethic in our country. While citizens of other cities do, those in the country's capital *Delhi-gate*!

Disclaimer: Delegation works very well in most places. But as they say in TV ads featuring motorcycle stunts, do not try delegating *at home*. Your wife is smarter than you think.

> 'When in doubt, mumble; when in trouble,
> delegate; when in charge, ponder.'
>
> —James H. Boren

All Hail the Excuse

Practising social distancing from the truth.

What happens after the game is over, the judgment has been passed and the moment of truth dawns? The victor can be expected to simper pearly platitudes—all of which you've heard before. But for novelty and spunk, turn to the other corner, to those who came second, third or last best. That's where you will meet wit, imagination and an iconoclastic disregard for fact. It's where you will find that masterpiece of the inventive mind—the excuse.

Apart from being a loser's best friend, the excuse is also a universal alibi. The Jharkhand neta who was caught literally with his pants down inside a railway compartment had his excuse ready—he had an upset stomach. Then there was the incident many years ago when CCTV cameras in the Karnataka Assembly Hall caught a couple of honourable ministers doing something not so honourable—watching porn even as the session was on. When the news broke, and the ministers realized that the smut had hit the fan, they were fazed only for a moment. Before you could say, Sunny Leone, they came back strongly with the line that they had been conducting research on the subject of depravity for a forthcoming seminar. This was further embellished to indicate that they were also jointly gathering material for a treatise on the exploitation of women. Such original ideas! Indeed, in their final moments, the ministers displayed greater agility of mind and intellectual incandescence than they ever did in office.

If excuses often bring out the best in us, it is probably because we have such long practice in developing them. Right from the tender days when we had to provide momma with plausible reasons why the number of laddoos had dwindled overnight we have been hardwired to find innovative ways of sidestepping blame. At school, we could make sci-fi seem colourless with homespun reasons for unfinished homework and unlearnt formulas. In the years since then, the part of the brain that forms excuses has been regularly exercised. Now you know how our Minister of Finance so fulsomely explains the sorry state of the country's finances time after time. The excuses cover a broad spectrum, ranging from 'the previous government's policies left a huge hole in the country's finances'; 'it's a global thing—other countries are suffering more than we are (doesn't that make us happy?)'; to the plucky counter-punch, 'our economy is actually doing splendidly. It's your shoddy method of calculation that needs to change.'

Excuses are the fig leaves we use to cover up facts, and as an inveterate excuser myself, I know how handy they can prove. I've lost count of the number of times they have helped me out of do-or-lie situations. It's not that I fancy the ornate excuse more than the honest truth—it's just that the world throws up many questions to which you don't know the answer or, worse, the answer is unknowable. What, for example, do I say when bowled existential googlies such as 'How could you do this?' or 'Tell me everything that happened!' Philosophers may say that excuses aren't durable and that the truth will come out in the end, but when you are in a hole, your immediate priority is to extricate yourself. As for the long term, we shall cross the bridge when we come to it.

Two decades ago, management pundit C.K. Prahalad popularized jugaad—the quick-fix solution that we Indians are supposed to be world champions at. Well, think of the excuse as the jugaad of human interaction—essential improvisations to keep the show going and the wheels of society moving. Stop for a moment and imagine the consequences if, by executive fiat, excuses were demonetized, so to speak. Everyone would have to admit to everything, causing much uproar and unpleasantness, serious loss of face and upsetting the social balance our forefathers did so much to put together. It will end up in a kind of lockdown that will make the last one seem like a ball.

You don't need to feel overly guilty about this habit of social distancing from the uncomfortable truth. After all, it's not as if you are out to play a con trick on some hapless innocent, or that you're saying anything with global ramifications. You are not, for instance, talking of anything like the mother of all excuses, 'weapons of mass destruction'. You are not being at your inscrutable best when asked about the origins of a pandemic. Your modest ambition is limited to extracting yourself from soup while losing as little personal dignity as possible.

I can bet the person listening to you probably knows an excuse when he (or more likely, she) hears one. But she is savvy enough to see the big picture, and considering the larger scheme of things, also likely to let you off lightly. After all, the show must go on.

I have this on fairly good authority, viz., William Shakespeare. In one of his more cerebral sonnets, he says: 'When my love swears that she is made of truth/I do believe her, though I know she lies.' Remember, he's the same guy who gave us 'All's well that ends well'.

> 'The eye is always caught by light,
> but shadows have more to say.'
>
> —Gregory Maguire

Managing Your Boss

A vital survival guide for these difficult days.

Author Vikram Seth and filmmaker Mira Nair may not know it, but the quest for a suitable boss has more twists and turns, more bumps and bends, than the manhunt for a suitable boy. One of the reasons this is such a tricky business is that bosses mutate (that's why there are no vaccines against them). Some are wise, some supervise; some mean well, others are, well, mean. There are bosses whom you look up to, and those you need to watch out for. Since you never know which of the above you are going to draw in the office lottery, it makes sense to be prepared for all of them.

Alas, management schools teach little more than finance, HR and marketing in their curriculum. They don't teach you the most vital skill of all—managing your boss. (Even sadder, Salman Khan doesn't tell you despite this being Season Umpteen of Big Boss.) So here, dredged from painful but gainful experience, are the lessons you need to learn.

The first thing you need to know is that bosses belong to another planet. When you are talking about antakshari, they will talk about opera; if you are describing a scuffle at the bus stop, they will turn to rising levels of intolerance across the world. If you complain about canteen food, they will tell you that an avocado or a spoonful of chyavanprash will meet all your nutritional needs. The sooner you understand this difference of perspective, the easier it will be for you to scramble up the rungs of the corporate ladder.

It's a common mistake to believe that these men or women from Mars are forever critical of what you think or do. In fact, bosses often like your idea—so much that they make it their own. That's why, the perspective plan you have slogged over for days will, with a few punctuations added, re-emerge from their desk. There won't be many visible changes but the initials at the bottom will be theirs. You ought to be happy. Appropriation is the sincerest form of flattery.

Next, learn to read your boss' mind. This is difficult, but it is not like getting hold of Don. '*Don ko pakadna mushkil hi nahin, namumkin hai.*' (Getting hold of Don is not only difficult but impossible.) All it needs are eagle eyes and the native ability to put two and two together. Extensive experience and acute observation will give you tell-tale indications of their ideological leanings, pet peeves, magnificent obsessions, soft spots and Achilles heels. Having all this pat is like having a Google Map of your boss' thought patterns. You are on sure ground when, as part of the time-honoured corporate ritual, your 'frank' opinion is sought on critical matters. This could include important things, such as selecting a name for the department's newsletter, the wallpaper for his cabin or the logo for the annual dealer meeting. Knowing his likely choices beforehand, you simply have to align your own view as closely as possible to his. You will then be thought to be an executive with taste and mature sensibilities. Ergo, a promotable executive.

Delegation comes naturally to bosses. A former boss once told me that when it comes to minor jobs, he delegates them to his juniors. When it comes to major jobs, he delegates them as well—for how else will the juniors learn? In effect, assignments slide off the boss like water off a duck's back. This is because most offices have adopted the social structure of bees. There's a queen bee, whose job is to simply lord it over the others while a swarm does the actual work of harvesting honey. (I believe that is why management schools are called 'B Schools'.)

HR manuals tell senior executives that they must walk the talk to win the approbation and respect of their juniors. Some bosses, however, have taken this literally to mean that they must be seen charging hither to thither, clocking 15 kmph in the stretch between the conference room and washroom, and then emerging to break the sound barrier in the home stretch to the cabin. You know and I know that there is precious little for him to do once he is inside the cabin. But when a boss acts busier than he is, who are you to puncture his pretence?

Similarly, if you discover that your boss is not the brightest bulb in the box, it will be hazardous to poke fun at his shortcomings, unless you have an attractive career option lined up as your Plan B. Dim as they are, they have sense enough to grasp that they are being made fun of behind their backs. They can hit back viciously. So it is much better to let nature take its course. The truth will out, and so will idiocy.

A common trait of bosses is that they play favourites. They have learnt this technique not from any of your elite management schools but from history books, which tell us about the stunningly effective 'divide and rule' policies of the Brits. You may be tempted to join the charmed circle of your boss, because being his favourite can mean a lighter work-load, fewer chances of incurring his wrath on a bad Monday morning and the prospects of being nominated to receive awards on behalf of the department (this will turn your colleagues greener than a jealous grasshopper). But remember, times change, and so will bosses. When a new boss takes over the reins, all the old favourites are automatically marked out as enemy agents. So if you are playing for the long innings, it is smart not to be seen as the boss' stooge—or to use the more astringent Hindi equivalent—'chamcha'.

Despite learning all these tricks of the trade listed here, you may still find yourself part of the swarm, not the queen. If that happens, make time for your ally and wait till the wheel turns full circle. Slowly, but steadily, you will move up the ladder, until one day, you hit upon the perfect boss—yourself.

> 'We celebrate originality and courage, but those who rise to the top are often conformists and sycophants. It's a painful lesson in how corporates operate.'
>
> —George Monbiot

Playing the Name Game

Dropping names is a passport to fame and success.

'My name is Bond, James Bond' should rank among the most iconic self-introductions ever. We may not all have a name as devastatingly sexy as 007's, but whether we are plain Janardhan, Murli or Bakulesh, most of us like the music in our names, and we are touchy about how they are pronounced. The Bard may have been dismissive, but I bet the world wouldn't have revered him so much and for so long if he had been plain old 'Bill'. Every part of the name carries its own significance. In India (except in advertising agencies and the IT industry), most people of a certain age and seniority are known by their surnames, while the humble office assistant is Raju to all. Although we recognize the importance of a name, we will never realize the wonders it can perform until we learn to drop them. In a world in which where you stand depends on whom you know, name-dropping is your passport to a higher social and professional status. It's an 'upgrade' from Economy through Business, straight to First Class. As a veteran name-dropper myself, I must confess that if I have gotten this far in life, there's a lot I owe to expertly lacing my conversations with entries drawn from the 'who's who' of society. From the Page 3 types to sports stars, right up to the cerebral celebrities who make it to the edit pages—all of them are in my database, and most of them are known by their first names. They have been my 'Open Sesame' to shut doors, given me the trappings of respectability and helped me (ahem) jump queues for everything, from vaccines to visas.

Before we go any further, we need to understand the subtle nuances that distinguish the surname from the first name and the first name from the optional, but high-value, nickname. The surname is public property, prefixed by Mr or Mrs or suffixed by 'ji', north of the Vindhyas. Anyone can use it. The first name, and even more so, the nickname, is a different ball game altogether. It carries with it connotations of familiarity and proximity. So when you are on a name-dropping mission, the name you need to try and employ is obviously the first. But hold on, there is still a lot to learn for there is much more to effective name dropping than just having a copious database that you dip into as and when the need arises. It needs finesse in deployment.

For instance, crash-landing into a conversation to announce that you have just met Mr Amitabh Bachchan is an amateur's way to go about it. It sounds boastful and crass and you are probably not going to be believed. A seasoned name dropper, however, would therefore opt for the 'doosra'—the trick delivery perfected by Pakistan's Saqlain Mushtaq. Here, you gently ease into an ongoing chat to say, 'Amitji said he enjoyed my child's watercolour painting.' (You can substitute watercolours with nursery rhymes, zumba or mimicry of hawkers' calls...anything will do for, as great artists say, the material is immaterial).

'Who?' your listeners ask, not sure if they heard it right.

'Oh, Amitji—Mr Amitabh Bachchan,' you explain. You have used your kid's watercolours (or whatever) as a decoy and made the name-drop seem almost incidental to the main story. You have also revealed that you know the star well enough to step over the Lakshman Rekha of the surname. It's a clever turn, and even Saqlain would have nodded in appreciation. Your stock will have zoomed to stratospheric heights.

There is some homework to be done before you begin rolling out the names of the rich and/or famous. To start with, draw up profile pictures of people whom you claim are your close friends and boon companions. If you are at a film club get-together, you can wow members by claiming that a leading Kolkata filmmaker is a dear family friend. If said filmmaker also happens to be in the hall and displays no sign of recognition, you will have a lot of explaining to do.

Discretion is the better part of a name dropper. If you claim to know everyone in the world, you diminish the value of those whom you do know. So make a judicious selection of the people who really matter. Also, as luck would have it, if you run into another of your ilk—a fellow name dropper at a party, don't fall into the temptation of trying to match ace for ace. You say you know the beat inspector well. He counters by saying that he knows the Superintendent, to which you could respond by saying that you are also on good terms with the DIG. This can spiral all the way to the top of the police hierarchy, and get neither of you anywhere. Far from impressing your audience, they will be sniggering at the spectacle.

Modern technology, as we all know, has two sides to it. On the one hand, it is a booster shot for name droppers seeking new pastures. Using social media, you can tag your posts to eminent names. It suggests, without explicitly stating, that we count a multitude of VIPs as friends. But technology can also bite. It has made information accessible to everyone with a smartphone. I can no longer casually claim, for instance, that I play golf every Sunday morning with the city's biggest business tycoon. Before I so much as complete the sentence, the local busybody will proffer proof that said tycoon does not play golf at all, and that his preferred sport is, in fact, dabba ice pice.

All this does not mean that the practice has stopped (we name droppers are made of sterner stuff). It only means that we need to watch our steps.

Looking at it objectively, if you are the type who believes in the sterling virtues of hard work and perseverance, you can plod your way to your goals, and good luck to you. Otherwise, simply drop the right names and you will be well on your way up. You will know you have arrived when the name that people drop is your own.

Dom Moraes was arguably one of India's finest poets in English. But a tendency to name-drop remained the good man's Achilles heel till the last. In an article in The Times of India, *while debating the work of a controversial writer, he thought it fit to say: 'Without wishing to drop names, I must add that a dead friend of mine, W.H. Auden, liked it too.' The riposte came soon enough. Mumbai (then Bombay) University professor, Vrinda Nabar, in a letter to the editor, delivered the coup de grace: 'When I don't wish to name-drop, I actually don't!'*

Life Lessons from Potholes

How to pave the road ahead with bliss.

We, Indians, ought to be thrilled by the romance of the rains, year after year. This is the moment to marvel. The lightning sets off flashbulbs in the sky and thunder rolls sonorously overhead—God's very own sound and light show.

Sadly, we do nothing of the sort. Instead of waxing lyrical about the pied cuckoo heralding the advance guard of the rain gods, we are more prosaic. We talk about potholes. Or rather, we begin talking…and then rapidly scale up to screaming, cussing and ranting vile abuse at our city fathers. This is an annual, unfailing occurrence, and there didn't seem to be a solution in sight until one evening, on the way back from work, I stumbled upon both—a pothole and a profound truth. I have now seen the light, and unstinting as ever, am prepared to share it with all those who want the road ahead to be paved with bliss.

You don't begin with the macadam—that will get you nowhere. Instead, you begin with the mind. You need to stop looking upon every bump as injurious to life and ligament. Steer clear of black humour too, desisting from the witty and withering—'that pothole linking Andheri to Powai has a road every few metres!' Instead, step right back, and tell yourself and anyone prepared to listen, that those potholes are here for a higher purpose.

What higher purpose can there be, you ask, to a puddle-filled hole, which tells you of the shoddy work of the municipal authorities and suggests a rosy-cosy nexus between officials and contractors? There has literally been dirty work at the crossroads. But calm down, calm down. As I said before, you need to train your mind to transcend mundane matters like money or municipality and view things from a grander, loftier perspective. When you look at it dispassionately, potholes are nature's way of telling us to slow down. Psychologists and gurus have been telling us the same thing, but a pothole is more persuasive. A life led continuously on the fast lane can have adverse consequences for the heart, apart from causing collateral damage to the soul. So ease up and let 20 km per hour be the pace at which you lead life.

A cratered road is also one of life's great levellers. It's where you in your autorickshaw can catch up with the BMWs and Mercs that had honked and zipped past you earlier. You can even smile sweetly at the occupants of those luxury limos, serene in your newfound knowledge that despite appearances, all men are equal. Or to put it in a more evocative local idiom—'you and me, same to same, brother.' Also, do not delude yourself into thinking that if you take a different route tomorrow, all will be well. Give and take a crater or two; all roads are the same. But that doesn't mean you throw in the towel and refuse to step out of your gated community. How long will you keep away?

As Don Quixote had said, albeit in a slightly different context, 'Those who halt at the inn, and call it quits, are missing the whole point of life. Realistically, there is no inn; it is the road now and forever—finite man probing infinity.'

Apart from helping you attain such dizzy heights of philosophy, potholes have a practical side too. They are a useful addition to your address. 'Take the first left,' I tell a friend while directing him home, 'after the horseshoe-shaped pit. You will soon see a black hole that the universe would have been proud to call its own. Get past that, and stop in front of a series of three interconnected potholes…and that's the Bima Nagar gate right there.' Once we accept that potholes are a part of life, we can go one better and proceed to market them. The idea is based on the tried and trusted dictum: if you can't beat them, brand them.

Let's consider repositioning the rough and tumble of our roads as an adventure course—a free roller-coaster ride with every commute. Or they could be promoted as pure entertainment. In which city in the world can you see heaving and swaying double-decker buses doing an item number? There's also the potential of alternative therapy—especially for effete tourists from abroad who have driven all their lives on autobahns and expressways, and who won't know a pothole until it hits them. Tourists out to see 'Incredible India' can get acupuncture on the go. You get from Point A to Point B even as your sluggish liver and clogged arteries are nudged into active mode with jolts, jabs, thumps and bumps.

Nobody really knows how many potholes the nation can actually lay claim to. Official figures are almost certainly as much of an undercount as Covid-positive figures in Uttar Pradesh during the peak of the pandemic. Perhaps we will know exactly where we stand if we adopt the excellent example of Nandan Nilekani's precedent-setting Personal Identification Number system. We can then give every bump on every road a unique 12-digit identity.

But on second thought, numerals are a cold, clinical way to describe something as touchy and feely as a pothole. Potholes need names—and what better than to christen them after your friendly neighbourhood trinity of corporators, civic officials and road contractors? I am sure the concept of branded potholes has the potential to transform your mindset from sullen acceptance to something bordering on affection. Think of the deliciously wicked kick you will get out of bumping over pits and cracks named after the very people who had contributed to creating them!

Suddenly, potholes won't seem such a bad thing after all.

'The road to success is always under construction.'

—Steve Maraboli

The Bald, Bold and Beautiful

Don't tear your hair about balding.

At a certain age many men and a few women begin to look at themselves in the mirror the way the world looked at Afghanistan after the Taliban took over—with mounting anxiety about what was going to happen next. And then, one day, solicitous scrutiny confirms our worst fears—we are going bald! It's the kind of rude self-realization that takes time to sink in. While there are other ways by which aging sends you its calling card like creaky joints, crinkly skin and shortness of breath, none of them seem as grievous as losing your locks.

Male pattern baldness is so common that it is almost inevitable, and it is only a matter of time before the whole world becomes bald. You then wonder what the fuss is all about. It's not as if you were Samson in the first place. But then, there's always the wistful thought of what might have been. Only the other day, or so it seems, we had a luxuriant top mop; we were just one swish of the comb away from being mistaken for Ayushmann Khurrana. Also, let's be honest, lurking inside even the most modest of men is the wellspring of vanity. Rather than resign ourselves to the pate worse than death, we resort to desperate camouflage. We strategically rearrange strands, dive head-first into essential oils and hair restorers or take to wearing a hat. None of this really works for long, and one is reminded of Charlie Chaplin saying that a man caught in an embarrassing situation is funny...but things get uproarious when he tries to pretend that everything is normal.

Much better than pretence is to follow the old maxim—'If you can't beat them, join them.' Many men grow bold even as they are getting bald, and carry out a pre-emptive strike. They shave their scalp before nature can get into the act. Apart from the pleasure of outsmarting ageing, the bald look has been considered quite attractive ever since Yul Brynner set the trend. But if your family and friends can't stand you looking like The Rock, minus the muscles, you need to try loftier methods of regaining your peace of mind.

What cannot be cured can be comforted. First of all, it's the early days that will seem the longest. You will think the whole world has banded together to stare at the space above your ears. You may even become the target of catcalls, featuring such unflattering but unforgettable terms as 'tubelight' and 'takloo'. But all this is a temporary phase, and you just need to get acclimatized. If time can heal broken hearts, what's a bald pate?

When you look at the bright side (excuse the pun), you realize that losing hair helps you gain some valuable life lessons. Simply put, what you lose on the outside, you gain on the inside, as you realize that accepting yourself as the person you are is the first step to inner peace. Relieved of the irksome burden of self-delusion and make-believe, you will experience the sense of lightness that happiness gurus and advertisers of laxatives go ga-ga about.

There's another advantage. Your lack of hair can be seen as a brand ambassador for all things cerebral—you now possess the wisdom born of long experience. Our society may be changing, but it hasn't yet changed so much that our people have stopped valuing seniority. If a weighty issue is being debated, most people would back the bald head over the long mane. 'Oh, that long-haired chap only looks cool,' they will say, 'but I doubt if he's ever used his brains.'

Generally, when you get thin at the top, you simultaneously go thick in the middle. Now, a ballooning waistline, more than an ebbing hairline, is actually something you need to get serious about. A paunch announces to the world that its owner lives, not wisely, but too well. It betrays your now-on, now-off fitness regimen and says that you tend to run amok with the dessert. But balding holds no such guilty associations.

There is also evidence to suggest that hair loss improves character. Those who have spent their youth preening themselves in front of a mirror become conscious of the impermanence of it all. As they say, 'hair today, gone tomorrow.' If you think that is a crude way of expressing a delicate sentiment, perhaps Franz Kafka would sound more poignant: 'Everything you love is very likely to be lost.'

Even if none of these pearls of wisdom brings you solace, don't get upset. And whatever you do, don't tear your hair. Alas, that's one response you will not be able to afford any more.

> 'Stupidity talks. Vanity acts.'
>
> —Victor Hugo

No Spitting, Know Spitting

The 'thoo', the whole 'thoo' and nothing but...

If you want to lead a comfortable life in India, you need to know about spitting—who does it, why they do it and how to escape unscathed and un-spat upon.

First, the back story: Early in April 2021, an advocate and activist in Mumbai filed a public interest litigation in the Bombay High Court against spitting in public. Their lordships acted with alacrity, and on April 7, issued a court order directing the police to take action. The time was opportune. The 'Me Too' movement had done its job, and it was now easy to name and shame predators, turning urban wildlife into passably well-behaved gentlemen. After 'Me Too', it was time for the 'Aak-thoo' movement to get into gear. Also, the pandemic had given a fresh lease of life to the attempt to stop Indians from throwing caution along with a million pathogens to the winds. But soon, the authorities came to know what they were up against. In India it was not a few leaks that they were trying to plug, they were trying to stop a spitsunami.

In India, spitting has a pedigree more impressive than the winners of dog shows. If you were to stoop and examine the long, dimly-lit corridors of our history, you would find them spattered in many hues, for we have been spitting for as long as we can remember. When India battled its colonial masters, Gandhi-ji had tried to rally the side, saying: 'If we Indians [in 1947, 390 million strong] could only spit in unison, we would form a puddle big enough to drown 300,000 Englishmen.' Well, the Quit India Movement is over, but the Spit India Movement continues in full flow. We have forgotten the harder lessons that the Mahatma taught us, like ahimsa and non-violence because it did not quite suit our native personality, but spitting suits us to the 'T'—or to the 'thoo'!

Spitting in public is India's great unifier, transcending the besmirched walls of religion, region and income. If the poor spit as they walk, the rich spit on the go. We've all seen owners of posh cars, slowing down a bit, rolling down the window pane and transferring the contents of their mouths onto the road. That's because spitting is a pan-India phenomenon, or more precisely, a paan-India thing. You don't need to hunt for proof—just look for the nearest corner or public wall to behold regurgitated folk art in the betel leaf medium. The betel leaf, accompanied by tobacco, plays a big role in promoting the spitting culture, and it has made its way into popular culture. Be honest—didn't we all watch with amusement as Big B intoned, '*Khaike paan Banaras wala [Oh to eat paan made in Benaras (now Varanasi)]*,' and spat spectacularly keeping time with the music?

You won't find many people abroad treating the world as their spittoon. The acid-veined V.S. Naipaul picked on this when he said, 'The Indian who has not travelled abroad cannot and does not know what civic cleanliness means, and so does not mind its absence.' But Naipaul, in his India-bashing mode, was more angry than accurate. A century before the writer had begun plying his trade, spitting was common in the US. All public places, including courtrooms, were provided with cuspidors—a fancy name for spittoons. The honourable judge had an exclusive cuspidor, not to be tainted by the rest of the world. Then things changed, and it took an illness to usher in a hygiene revolution. Tuberculosis broke out across the country and widespread cases led to a vigorous campaign to outlaw the act of spitting. It was the call America needed to turn over a new leaf. We Indians frequently turn over a new leaf too—only it's the betel leaf.

We seem to have received social sanction for our actions. This means we are not furtive spitters who look around to see if anyone is watching before hastily letting fly. On the other hand, we spit as if we relish the full process, accompanied by appropriate sound effects at every stage—from the deep gurgle to the climactic splash. Since the thoo, the whole thoo and nothing but the thoo is going to be an integral part of our lives, we need to learn to make our peace with it. What better than thinking positively?

If you look at things from the spitter's point of view, you will agree, for instance, that there is much to be spat at in our country. Reading the newspapers, watching TV and looking at the state of affairs, spitting is a spontaneous natural reaction—often the only one possible.

Another way of looking at spitting is as a punctuation mark. Frequent spitters don't spit as a sign of disgust or because there is phlegm lodged in their gullet. It is a method of assisting the listener in comprehension. When you are narrating a long story, it helps mid-sentence to turn around and spit. It's the non-verbal equivalent of 'do you get what I am saying?'

Spitting also functions as a convivial social gesture. We are social creatures, and sometimes we spit because everyone in our circle is doing it. You don't want to look like the odd man out and appear stand-offish.

Last but not least, spitting is self-defence. If as the experts say, your sputum can hold all manner of toxins, imagine how dangerous it would be for me to retain that unholy cocktail in my system! Better safeguard myself by diffusing it around now and again, and good luck to those passing by.

While the new rules issued by the authorities are welcome, the question is who will ensure that they are implemented on the ground? Alas, the guardians of the law themselves are not above occasionally turning aside from conversation, cupping their mouth, and…aak-thoo!

It could prompt you and me to turn around and say: Et thoo, Brute!

'If men spit upon the ground, they spit upon themselves.'

—Chief Seattle of the Suquamish and Duwamish tribes

Becoming an Expert

If you want to lead a healthy life, walk.
If you want to lead a happy life, swagger.

After studying the world for years and tracking who's what, I have stumbled upon a secret. The cushiest job in the world is being an expert. In the rough and tumble journey that we call life, experts are the ones who travel first class.

Which precise field do you become an expert in? Well, at the office, you can take your pick from environment conservation, corporate strategy, brand management, cold fusion or artificial intelligence. At home, the palate of possibilities is even wider. It includes mastery in everything, from Vaastu through barbecue to the best way of clearing dog poo. You can even strike a topical note by becoming an expert in pandemics—how to spot it, how to stop it. Actually, it matters little which domain you choose, because the steps to becoming an expert are more or less the same.

Is it hard work? The short answer is it's up to you. If you choose the straight and narrow path, you will need to invest long hours in study. It involves working for long periods, and you can never quite be sure of a favourable outcome. Alternatively, you can opt out of the drudgery and choose the method of becoming the most popular expert, viz., simply assume you are one already.

The advantages are many and mouth-watering. If you succeed in becoming an expert in the office, you can get colleagues of a lesser God to do all the heavy lifting. Minions will fact-check, proof-check, organize the back room, arrange for coffee and cookies and take care of the million little things that you, the expert, can't be bothered with. This ethnic cleansing of the minutiae of life frees up your mind for the grander tasks no one else is equipped to perform.

As an expert you need to literally walk the talk. Try walking about a foot above mean sea level, and make sure to advertise your stature. Mike Tyson used to say he won many of his bouts as he walked towards the ring. It would pay to do a Tyson walk at the office or your next family gathering. An air of self-assurance and superiority, with a thinly veiled threat to annihilate anyone who crosses your path—all come in handy.

Experts also speak a different tongue from the herd—it's the language of, well, other experts. You don't try and guess what's going to happen in the future. Instead, you study trends and develop a probability matrix. You don't just surf the net and download useful stuff; you carry out a wide, brand-agnostic survey and offer an assessment. And you never say that you had just happened to be at the right spot at the right time. Or that you got lucky with a sudden idea. You worked on it over the weekend and discovered implications that lesser minds had missed.

A vital skill is learning to speak without giving away too much. Just suppose you—the expert in gardening—are asked by admirers gushing over your chrysanthemums about the best way to get these blooms in their backyards. Your response shouldn't dwell on the nitty-gritty of soil, seed or season. That's small stuff. Instead, you will put on a faintly bored expression (you've been asked this question a million times by your fans before), and unleash an abstract profundity. 'Learn to talk to your flowers,' you will say, 'then…listen quietly till they talk back to you.'

There are experts who opt for a strategy contrary to talking in airy-fairy terms like a poet on pot. They become intimidatingly exact and numb their audience with numbers.

In place of saying that productivity in small and medium enterprises is falling (anyone could have said that), you need to say that it has dropped by 11.32 percentile in the last quarter. Before somebody has the time to google it, you step further out of the line and add a rider—of course, it doesn't include the figures for ancillaries because the data is not yet in.

Whatever you do, bear in mind that you can't afford to err like ordinary humans. This is not as difficult as it seems. Infallibility is easy—provided you leave an escape route just in case things don't go as per script. For instance, if the discussion turns to digital communications, you, the expert in social media, can create quite a stir by predicting the imminent death of a popular social media platform. Your listeners will be gobsmacked.

'Phew!'

'You don't say!'

'Are you sure, but…?'

You smile mysteriously, nod knowledgeably and add the fine print—unless someone somewhere does something different. That's the kind of 'black swan' escape clause that will help extricate you from the stickiest of situations and maintain your cent per cent strike rate.

Experts have a love-hate relationship with publicity; they pretend to hate it but secretly love it. They will duly turn their noses up at PR agents and say that their work speaks for itself. But that's only for the record. They are actually as hungry as you and I to get their names and mugshots in the papers, on television and online. After all, even experts are human.

You can help your PR guy along by cultivating the look you require. Appearances count a lot. Imagine if Zubin Mehta looked like The Great Khali. He wouldn't even be allowed into the world's stately concert halls, let alone be invited to conduct the orchestra. And I think I know why our former Reserve Bank chief Raghuram Rajan's popularity spread far beyond the staid portals of the bank. He managed to be intelligent without looking owlish. Just imagine if our central bank was in the hands of someone looking like a Taliban tribal chief!

The truth is that your hairstylist, tailor, dermatologist and cosmetic surgeon have a bigger role in manufacturing experts than all the tutorials and TED Talks you may attend or address. Bear in mind, however, that experts and Rome have one thing in common—they were not built in a day. Your 'expertise' is first recognized by your immediate circle, then by distant acquaintances, and so on until you become a household name. Till then, hang on—becoming an expert is well worth the wait.

> 'Men prefer to believe that they are degenerated angels rather than elevated apes.'
>
> —William Winwood Reade

Dealing with 'Meeting-itis'

Causes, symptoms and cures.

'Meeting-itis' is an affliction that's been around for so long that you could dismiss it as being endemic and not worth your immediate attention. But the pandemic and its aftermath have given rise to a trickier, more toxic variant—the virtual or online meeting. Whichever strain you contract, the symptoms are the same. 'Meeting-itis' makes people feel the urge to meet and talk animatedly about work, rather than sit bored all by themselves at work.

Why do people meet? Well, that's like asking why people fall in love. Human instinct, I guess. Man has always regarded an assembly of five or more with respect. This is based on our deep-seated belief that if two heads are better than one, then three should be better than two, and so on. There are also excellent historical references going back to our fabled past. It took our cave-dwelling forefathers a meeting around the fire to decide the next day's menu as well as to take steps to prevent themselves from featuring in the menu of the sabre-toothed tiger. From those formative years, the meeting has grown steadily in importance till we have reached the point when almost nothing you say or do is taken seriously unless you have video conferenced, 'zoomed' or 'teamed'.

Modern man knows that there is more to a meeting than meets the eye. We now see it as an officially sanctioned effort-saving device. Until just over a decade ago, to shirk work you needed to suddenly fall ill, lose a near relative or think of some other cataclysm to visit your household. But now, there are meetings that save you from taxing your imagination. On the morning that you feel disinclined for work, and such mornings are becoming common, you call for a meeting. You will find ready acceptance because a lot of your colleagues in other departments may also be simultaneously experiencing similar disinclinations. The obvious solution: a teleconference. How can we forget that at the peak of the 'work from home' era, the meeting was a godsend? Unless your spouse was cued in and knew exactly what was going on, a 'very important office meeting' could save you from a dozen sundry errands—peeling onions, clearing the loft and putting your desk in order.

The meeting is also a marker of status. Tell me about the meetings you attend, and I will tell you where you stand in the office hierarchy. Only people of importance attend meetings, and the more important you are, the more of them you attend. Indeed, right at the apex, it's back-to-back meetings all the way. Lightweights don't get a look-in. So when young executives are asked to join a meeting comprising their seniors, they can barely conceal their pride. Conversely, if you find your name missing from the list of invitees sent around a day earlier, you have been effectively dropped from the 'A' team. If you want to know how to overcome such disappointment, ask Ajinkya Rahane. He is a veteran in this department.

As important as the number of meetings you clock is the size of the meeting. If there are just two or three of you sitting around a table, all you are doing is having coffee and a conversation. There is no point going around claiming you are having a meeting. At the other end of the scale, if the assembly is very large and nearly everyone in the department is present in the conference hall, the importance of the meeting gets diffused, and like Kashmir, it loses its special status. A right-sized meeting involving the right kind of quality people is what you should be aiming at. It is also an excellent platform to demonstrate what the HR department would call 'the chain of command'. Or in plain speak, to show people who's boss. As soon as the meeting starts, you turn to the most pliant junior and tell him or her to 'take the minutes'. This will show your superiors how seriously you view these meetings and will also keep uppity juniors in their place.

Nobody really expects concrete results or definitive outcomes from a meeting. So once you have settled down, you can proceed with your normal routine—munch cookies, sip coffee and relax. A health warning here: the walls have antennas and the powers that be are sure to get to know about your passive performance. Don't be surprised then if you find yourself dropped from the next meeting. To pre-empt such a tragic turn of events, at least nod intelligently or ask harmless questions now and again, and pretend to take down a few points. For best results, you can't do better than revisit Shepherd Mead's classic, with its self-explanatory title *How to Succeed in Business Without Really Trying: The Dastard's Guide to Fame and Fortune.*

Many people have railed against the unproductiveness of it all. American writer Dave Barry once said, 'If you had to identify, in one word, the reason why the human race has not achieved, and never will achieve, its full potential, that word would be "meetings".'

America's former ambassador to India, John Kenneth Galbraith, put it more crisply, saying, 'Meetings are indispensable when you don't want to do anything.'

But whatever these wise men may say, I, for one, believe that 'meeting-itis' will outlive its critics, and survive far into the future. If you hold a different point of view and would like to present your case...why, let's have a meeting.

> 'Remember that sometimes not getting
> what you want is a wonderful stroke of luck.'
>
> —Dalai Lama XIV

Getting Wise to Good Advice

In from one ear, out from the other.

If the saddest words in the language are 'what might have been', the second saddest is 'I told you so'. Accompanied by much finger-wagging and expressions of disapproval, they hit you when you are down. There you are, kicking yourself and cursing your luck, when the person whose carefully curated words of advice you had cast to the winds turns up to rub salt into your wounds for not doing as you were told.

I, for one, have been sceptical about advisors ever since I heard what happened when Eve followed the serpent's recommendations. What a heavy price we've all been paying for an apple! Since then, advisors have gone forth, multiplied and expanded their scope of services. For instance, I run into a volley of unsolicited advice whenever I face any of life's large-, small- or medium-sized dilemmas. The powers-that-be also step in to guide me on dress, diction, destiny and why dhokla makes a better snack than dahi-vada.

Don't get me wrong. By and large, advisors are nice people—well-meaning, upstanding and water-drinking. But they are proud of their wellspring of wisdom and tend to rate it much higher than the market does. So when you flout their counsel, you are not merely disagreeing with them on some matter of academic interest, but also nuking their ambitions to be seen as a philosopher and guide. Hell, we are told, knows no fury like a woman scorned—but an unheeded advisor is likely to run close.

As things stand, advice is easier to give than to receive. Do a head count, and you will find that the total number of advisors in the world far exceeds the number of the 'advised'. Obviously, much of the advice currently in the system has found no takers, and many among us are following the excellent example of Oscar Wilde who said, 'I always pass on good advice. It is the only thing to do with it. It is never of any use to oneself.' It would certainly be more useful if actions spoke as loud as words—but they rarely do. Say, you find yourself in a jam, and so you approach the friendly neighbourhood counsellor for money. He will talk to you at length about the need for smart financial planning and remind you that if you had taken up the SIP he had recommended months ago, you wouldn't have gotten into this hole. You nod in agreement. It's excellent advice certainly, but even before he has finished speaking, you sense that you are not going to get so much as a rupee out of this party.

You don't need much skill to advise others—in fact, competence may often prove to be a hindrance. All of us, for instance, advise our netas on how the country ought to be run, and every workplace has disgruntled souls who claim they can do a far better job than the company management. As for cricket, we have a billion experts freely providing expertise to captain, batter, bowler and twelfth-man. Back at home, no family is complete without the greying eminence guiding you on the career path you should opt for and the spouse you should select. If you listen to these venerable words of advice, you may fail spectacularly. And if you pay no heed, you may fail all the same.

So what should you do? Play it safe and follow directions the way good motorists follow the GPS? Or make your own road?

On that point, alas, there is, and indeed there can be, no single right answer. In this lottery we call life, which piece of advice is going to click and which will go kaput is anybody's guess. If you follow your heart, and things still go wrong, you forfeit the chance to blame someone else. But who knows, you could be a better person for attempting to fly solo. In the liberating words of Pablo Neruda, 'You start dying slowly […]/ If you do not go after a dream/If you do not allow yourself/At least once in your lifetime/To run away from sensible advice...'

> 'I always advise people to never give advice.'
>
> —P.G. Wodehouse

Sleeping on the Job

The siesta finally wins a PR battle.

Let's face it. We are a sleep-starved society. Except for infants and the retired elderly, few of us regularly get our allotted eight-hour quota. By now, we ought to have been protesting this cruel deprivation, storming the palatial offices of the authorities in charge of these things and burning effigies of the gods and goddesses of sleep, and Kumbhakarna too for good measure. The reason why we haven't been driven to such extremes is that we've all along had a love–hate relationship with the activity, or more precisely, the inactivity called sleep.

I think it all stems from the negative brand image of sleep. As opposed to wakefulness, slumber (it even sounds like 'lumber') is taken as a sign of lazy indifference to responsibility that, as everyone knows, is the first step on the slippery slope to becoming an absolute good-for-nothing. The fact that some of the world's most revered personalities have pitched in to endorse it hasn't helped matters. Shakespeare, for instance, had waxed lyrical, calling sleep the 'balm of hurt minds… and chief nourisher in life's feast'. For all the Bard's eloquence, what prevails is something as yucky as 'the early bird catches the worm'.

Right from our schooldays, the child who rose bright and early was held up as a role model for all of us napping on the backbenches. The stigma associated with sleep has continued to stalk us all through. The heroes of popular culture are driven men and women who, while in mission mode, could survive on just a couple of hours of sleep. At the other end of the spectrum is the fat 'sleepy Joe' of Charles Dickens. The boy would snore even when he was standing. Your ideal citizen doesn't doze off while on duty. They are God-fearing, water-drinking, tax-paying, periodically vaccinating…and early-rising. Having risen, they will remain alert all through the day, fighting off sleep with the epic heroism of Lakshman repulsing the entreaties of Nidra while on vanvas-duty.

Of the two evils, sleeping at night vis-a-vis dozing in the afternoon, the latter is paradoxically seen as more inexcusable, although it is much shorter, and generally not in a prone position. Obviously, it suffers from a bigger image problem. Sir Winston Churchill tried to mould public perception by claiming that he converted one day into two by sleeping in the afternoon. Incidentally, he also won the war for the Allies, but that didn't get him very far. American social psychologist James Maas coined the term 'power nap' to rebrand the siesta and give it the appearance of a productivity booster. Also, research studies by NASA, no less, have demonstrated that a midterm snooze is a tonic for your mind. It improves verbal memory, motor skills and perceptual learning. Try telling all this to an anti-napper. They will just yawn.

I concede that one of the things going against us is human nature. People who are awake somehow feel morally superior to those who are asleep. As Jerome K. Jerome said, 'I don't know why it should be […] but the sight of another man asleep in bed when I am up, maddens me. It seems to me so shocking to see the precious hours of a man's life […] being wasted in a mere brutish sleep.' And then there is the aesthetics of it all. We certainly do not look our best when we slip into the land of Nod while we're seated. Of the many poses we unconsciously adopt, the most ungainly is the one where our mouth is agape, head tilted as far as it will go and legs stuck in embarrassingly awkward angles. Seeing such a spectacle at the front office can be bad for business. At a bank counter, for instance, it may put off customers who believe—

albeit mistakenly—that their money will be left unguarded while the staff catch their forty winks.

Mercifully, change seems to be in the air, and the powers-that-be are slowly waking up—excuse the pun—to the immense benefits of sleeping on the job. Credit goes to the millennials and their preference for work-life balance over bank balance and flexitime over inflexible office convention. For their part, bosses too show newfound respect for the Japanese practice of inemuri—literally, 'sleeping while present'. In the land of the rising sun, it is supposed to be a badge of honour to fall asleep during meetings for it shows that you have been burning midnight oil by the gallon.

Recently, an Indian company responded to the mood of the times by putting a stamp of approval on the afternoon nap. Employees get up to thirty minutes to sleep every afternoon. This 'daily doze' has been touted as the biggest boon the working classes have been able to wrest from the management since the invention of the casual leave. But not everyone is jumping about with joy at the news. Many say that it is only providing regulatory approval for something they used to do undercover anyway. I have a grouse too. The siesta somehow loses its charm when it is granted official sanction. Like kisses, the snooze is sweetest when it is stolen.

A study in the prestigious Psychology Today *found that late risers are likely to be more intelligent than their counterparts who prided themselves on getting up with the lark. So draw the blanket up, and sleep contentedly for that extra half hour. You have been proven right.*

Winning the 'Cold' War

What cannot be cured must be put to good use.

There are times in the year when almost everyone you know is either recovering from the common cold or is snivelling, coughing and periodically going...'akshoo!' Yet no pharma giant in the world has thought it fit to develop a sure-fire remedy. Worse, I don't see anyone trying.

Until the pandemic struck, the common cold used to be given—for want of a better word—step-doctorly treatment. Noses were turned up at runny noses, coughs fell on deaf ears and a sore throat that made you sound, albeit temporarily, like Big B, was dismissed as another Bollywood flop. It was believed that if you were aatmanirbhar enough, you should be able to cure a cold all by yourself in a matter of days.

Research says that the earliest human beings to catch a cold lived during the Iron Age. That was over three thousand years ago, and since then, there have been no signs of improvement. Once you accept the cold as a thing you cannot change, it makes sense to look for some benefit that you can derive from the situation.

So here are some tested ways to get the common cold to serve the common good. First, the cold is a malingerer's dream. Every time I needed a break from the office, I would advertise my condition by coughing sonorously within the boss' earshot. It made her stay away from my seat, fearing infection, and it gave me a cast iron alibi to phone in sick the next day. By sheer coincidence, that 'next day' could well be the day of the IPL finals.

In addition to trying standard issue allopathy, homoeopathy and naturopathy... the cold responds dramatically to 'serendipathy'. This is the gift of chancing upon remarkable cures while browsing WhatsApp. The common cold has democratized medical expertise so well that you too can become an instant expert. No technical knowledge is needed as you muster a large, respectful audience by recommending a spoonful of honey mixed with lime, a bit of ginger and garlic, mustard in milk, onion juice and chicken soup...the more exotic the herbs, the more respectful the audience. If it works, you have cemented your reputation for wonder cures. If it doesn't, just tell your 'patients' to be patient.

Yoga ranks among the trending methods to combat a cold. The explanation given by practitioners makes sound sense. The stretches and postures send breath, which has been cruising aimlessly around your system, to rush into the affected parts of your body and deliver a knockout punch to the cold virus. Of course, asanas are not as easy as Baba Ramdev makes it out to be, but look at it this way: you win a number of brownie points. You avoid loading your system with chemicals, you reconnect with India's ancient heritage and you are giving a thumbs-up to our government's efforts to popularize 21 June as International Yoga Day.

The best cure I have saved for the last. Few other illnesses can boast of having alcohol touted as a remedy. We've been told that 'A good gulp of whisky at bedtime— it is not very scientific, but it helps.' It's not just me saying it, that is Alexander Fleming, and his credentials are not to be sneezed at. The anti-inflammatory property of brandy is also supposed to reduce pain in sore throats and help in clearing congestion. While brandy and whisky are officially recommended, with some coaxing of the conscience, this can be stretched to include anything available in your bar. There are those amongst us who, not wishing to leave anything to chance, consume alcohol regularly as a preventive. Why take the risk?

With so many things going for it, I think the common cold deserves better. The advertising industry has all along been doing its bit to promote cold medication, but I feel that it hasn't gone far enough. We have seen TV spots showing loving mothers spoon-feeding cough syrup to their kids or applying balm to banish chest congestion. However, the agencies seem to have overlooked the romantic angle. When a boy loves a girl and vice versa, they won't mind risking infectious proximity to protect each other from the cold. This could be the start of a relationship both therapeutic and beautiful. Else, when the groom and bride decide to say 'I Do', they could add, unbidden, a high-decibel, 'AKSHOO!'

'A family is a unit composed not only of children but of men, women, an occasional animal and the common cold.'

—Ogden Nash

Minding our Ps and Queues

Who will cast the first stone
at queue-jumpers?

We all remember Amitabh Bachchan's sonorous, '*Hum jahan khade ho jaate hain, line wahin se shuru hoti hain*' (wherever I stand, the line begins with me). Long before Big B said it, however, we Indians had been practising what he preached. Granted, we may not all have put it into words because we lack the required baritone, but the impulse certainly runs strong. To cut a long line short, we always want the queue to begin with us.

It is not that we are inveterate breakers of rules. We just don't recognize that there is a rule there in the first place. Also, it's not as if we look down condescendingly upon those gentle folk who dutifully wait their turn at bus stops, billing counters in malls, airport check-in counters, etc. In fact, we hold them in high esteem and wish them well. It's just that our need is greater than theirs and our time more precious.

In major Indian cities, including and especially in Delhi, everyone firmly believes that rules are for fools and queues are for the clueless. So you take your place at the top of every queue by bovine right. When you think of it, you realize that queues are against the natural order that governs God's creatures, great and small. Ants may win our hearts by remaining in single file most of the time, but once a sugar crumb is nigh, it's every ant for itself. After the kill is done, do you ever see a pride of lions standing in a queue to feed itself? Or turn to another equally fearsome pride, viz., Mumbai commuters? With its nearly twenty million inhabitants, Mumbai is a city piled high on an island. If everyone were to stand in queue, many of us would be lost at sea.

So where did this weird practice—of standing in proximity to a total stranger and allowing more strangers to blow social distancing to bits—originate? I believe the queue, along with a lot of other undesirables, is a colonial hangover. That's why I don't find an exact equivalent for it in any of our mother tongues. As for the Brits, they love queues—in fact, they probably like standing in line even more than what they are going to get at the end of it. It stems from their obsession with regulation, order, discipline, etc., so alien to our native sense of spontaneity. Apparently, the line of people waiting for a final glimpse of Queen Elizabeth II lying in state at Westminster Hall was close to five miles—the world's longest queue. Phew! Well, who can argue with taste?

We Indians, however, know how to put our time to more productive use. We devise methods of short-circuiting a time-consuming process that is prone to human intervention. An obvious way is to brazen your way to the railway station's booking window while elbowing out other contenders. If you are lacking in the requisite brawn, get your brains to fill in. You can stroll towards the head of the queue, intently gazing at your WhatsApp, and ignore the feeble noises of protest around you. Cometh the hour, cometh the long jumper inside you.

An even more refined technique is to walk towards the booking clerk with an officious expression and a sheaf of papers. Most people are impressed by the trappings of authority and cave in meekly. Sometimes, you don't need to do anything spectacular. As luck would have it, you chance upon an 'old friend' ahead in the line, and sustain that bond until your purpose is served.

But in moments of quiet contemplation, even a queue-jumper like me of long-standing—or rather not standing—experiences pangs of guilt. As I said earlier, we are not incorrigible breakers of rules. The uncomfortable question we then ask ourselves is: Are we doing something wrong? Are we depriving the meek and the uncomplaining of their due? It is a disquieting thought, and it nagged at me for quite a while until I trumped it with another larger question—isn't the whole world guilty in one way or another? Aren't we all queue-jumpers in sheep's clothing?

Each of us is trying to get ahead in a race that was never meant to be fair or equal. Look around us. The privileged benefit from a hereditary head start. Their parents and grandparents have done all the queue-jumping necessary so that subsequent generations get easy access to position, power and pelf. Or turn to our career goals. They sound noble and nice at first but strip them of their HR fluff and pretence, and they are all sugar-coated ways to steal a march over the competition. For when you come down to it, what is 'networking' but a polished, socially-palatable term for queue-jumping? Let's face it. We are all guilty to a greater or lesser extent. An old Hindi saying puts it best: *'Iss hamam main sab nange hain'* (In this public bath, we all stand naked).

Ah, here comes the bus, and conscience placated to the extent possible, I take my rightful place. Queue E D!

> 'Everyone behaves badly—given the chance.'
>
> —Ernest Hemingway

In Praise of Praise

Why is it so difficult to say 'Shabash'?

Some people are so miserly with praise that the only way to get a decent compliment out of them is to pick up third-degree techniques from your nearest police station. What makes them skimp so much when a 'shabash' here and a 'well done!' or 'good job' there won't cost them a rupee? And why do they persist with their miserliness when guru after guru has said that a pat on the back is a powerful motivator?

My own DIY psychoanalysis tells me that it all boils down to jealousy. These guys are obviously seething with so much unexpressed envy that they can't stand someone else feeling good about what they have done. I also know of people—the stiff-lipped, starchy types—who actually pride themselves on being difficult to please. It is vicarious vanity and an oblique way of letting you know that their standards are lofty. If your benchmark is Sindhu, you can't be seen complimenting some stripling playing badminton at the society clubhouse.

But psychologists tell us that there is more to this

kanjoosgiri with compliments than meets the eye. There are those who start each day with a negative disposition. It is probably vinegar that runs through their veins, and changing their fundamental attitude to life would probably call for hospitalization and a long transfusion procedure. Sometimes, just sometimes, the causes are not so ignoble.

Apparently, some people don't like to be seen as flattering. So they go to the other extreme, and as they say, 'damn with faint praise'. Then there are those who believe that compliments breed complacency—pat someone on the back and pronto, the fire goes out of their belly. It's almost as if they are doing you a favour by criticizing you. If you ask me, all of them are rickety excuses. It's like refusing to give someone a lift in your car on a wet morning so that he learns for himself the benefits of carrying an umbrella.

There is one thing worse than not praising you; and that is praising someone else—in your presence. This is meanness topped with mischief. Shakespeare would have called it 'the most unkindest cut of all'. The person being praised could be your counterpart (ouch!), your cousin (ouch again) or—in a worst-case scenario—your rival. There is a word for it –'negging'. Vicious though it is, it's surprisingly common at work, at home and anywhere in between, and the perpetrators are otherwise very decent folk. But still, you won't get a good word out of them.

Over the years, and after many 'negging' sessions, I have learnt to develop my own homespun antidote to this form of criticism. When my boss pointedly tells me that Purshottam is the one who really knows how to prepare a report, respond to enquiries or think out of the box…I hear him out and then, smiling blandly, say something—anything—complimentary about the boss's counterpart (and closet rival) sitting in the next cabin. You could try the same trick with your wife—if you dare.

But as I've said before, we need not be scheming and squabbling with each other for praise. We need to accept that most of us are hardwired to like good things said about ourselves. We didn't need Abraham Maslow to spell out the hierarchy of needs and tell us that human beings crave appreciation even more than we crave money. Didn't we know that as children? A 'shabash' from papa or momma meant the world to us. Over the years, we may have outgrown the people we need praise from, but we haven't outgrown the need.

Once you have made up your mind to loosen your mental purse strings and be more liberal with your compliments, it is important to craft them well, and praise with finesse. Telling the wife (whom you have not complimented in aeons) that she looks like Deepika Padukone or the protagonist of the latest Netflix thriller is going wildly over the top. It could get your wife thinking about what your motives really are. Instead of allusions to film stars, you are more likely to hit the mark with a measured, 'That pale pink sari really suits you…it sets off your complexion.'

Better than scatter shooting, i.e., offering an all-encompassing compliment, it is better to be specific. This means that instead of a sweeping and generalized, 'Thank you for a wonderful dinner', you would fare better if you plunge into details. 'That baingan bharta was delicious. I know it's very difficult to get the consistency right, and this was perfect.' Your hostess will be a lot more pleased than if your compliment was vaguely positive. The only thing, make sure that brinjal was actually on the menu.

Obviously, being too free with your praises and showering them unthinkingly is to devalue your opinion and sense of discernment. Striking the fine balance between being a Scrooge with praise and being over-liberal is something you will learn with practice.

'I can live for two months on a good compliment.'

—Mark Twain

And Finally...

When life bowls a bouncer or an unplayable googly,
just pray you are at the non-striker's end.

As I said at the start, this book won't give you a bulletproof vest against stress and distress. If you can acquire happiness as easily as by reading a few hundred pages, you will probably lose it just as quickly. All this book does is to help you look at the world, and yourself, differently.

So let's not get overambitious, even in our aspirations for happiness. You can become miserable just thinking about why you are not happier than you already are. Or you can begin to wonder why other people, much less deserving, seem to be so joyous every time you meet them. That's a recipe for lifelong unhappiness. Instead, if you aim for, achieve and sustain a medium level of contentment most of the time, that should be as good as it gets. As the Jains do, say *'Michhami Dukkadam'* to all those around you—make peace with your past and move on.

If none of the above works, play your trump card: laugh. You can honestly say you had the last laugh.

Acknowledgements

My friends suggested that I write this book. I think they love to see me make a fool of myself!

Some of them have been friends since school, and others joined in later. They are too numerous to name, and each of them is too dear to risk missing out on any. But they will know whom I mean.

Thanks to Raj, Mano and the fabulous family I am blessed with, who took me at my word when I said I was a 'writer'. It absolved me of all the responsibilities of a normal human being.

I thank Rita Rahimtoola and John Monteiro—bosses willing to put a lot on the line when giving a callow youth a column to write in L&T's monthly magazine. Articles in the column were the seeds for this book. I can't forget Dorothy for her blessings despatched almost every evening from New York, which must certainly have helped speed up this book.

My proverbial 'big break' came years ago in *The Times of India*. I may not have quite lived up to the promise and leapt to higher orbits, but my gratitude to Bachi Karkaria and Jug Suraiya for helping put my name in print.

I thank M.S. Pinto, my school teacher, who evolved into a close family friend. He once told me to graduate from writing for corporates to writing for myself. I have done it now, sir. Shenaz, thank you for helping me with the proofs and demonstrating that you continue to be as meticulous as ever.

Thanks to Dibakar Ghosh at Rupa. On first reading of the manuscript, Dibakar had told me he had become a fan. I hope the fandom is durable. And thanks to my editor Shatarupa Dhar for blowing to bits my carefully cultivated illusion that I don't make mistakes in writing. May your eagle eye embellish shelf-loads of books.

Every year, at Mumbai's winter marathon, there are hundreds who stand on the side of the road and shout encouragement. I don't know if their 'buck up' and 'come on' actually helps the runners, but all of you have certainly made a world of difference to me in this long race of mine.

I have left for the end, a dear friend no longer around. He was my sounding board—from the first article to the last. He had read the final piece cheerfully and courageously while being laid low by a racking lung infection. Up there, I see Mukesh smiling encouragement.

www.ingramcontent.com/pod-product-compliance
Lightning Source LLC
Chambersburg PA
CBHW020329170426
43200CB00006B/325